89

For the Love of Alberta

Ways to Save Your Natural Heritage

Private Conservancy Guide for Alberta

Lesley Patricia Curthoys

Book design and illustrations by Rusty Brown
Front cover photograph by Howard Fix

First Edition

Canadian Cataloguing in Publication Data

Curthoys, Lesley Patricia, 1962-
    For the love of Alberta: ways to save your natural
heritage: private conservancy guide for Alberta

Includes bibliographical references.
ISBN 0-9696134-1-5

    1. Nature conservation--Alberta--Citizen
participation. 2. Conservation of natural resources--
Alberta--Citizen participation. 3. Nature conservation--
Alberta. 4. Conservation of natural resources--Alberta.
I. Federation of Alberta Naturalists. II. Title.

QH77.C3C87 1998   333.7'2' 097123   C98-900212-8

Published by the Federation of Alberta Naturalists
P.O. Box 1472
Edmonton, Alberta T5J 2N5
Fax (403) 453-8553

While this publication is designed to give accurate,
authoritative information, neither the author nor the
Federation of Alberta Naturalists renders legal or
financial advice. The reader should consult with
experienced professional advisors for specific and
current legal information.

Printed in Canada on 100% recycled paper.

This book is dedicated to
my parents,
Doris and Gerry Curthoys,

and to the memory of
Veronika Whitfield.

Contents

Acknowledgements

From the initial idea to the final product, this publication has been a team effort. Many people dedicated to protecting our natural heritage generously shared their thoughts, stories, photographs and expertise. Without their help, *For the Love of Alberta* could not have been produced.

And so, to the following people—and to anyone I may have inadvertently forgotten to mention—I thank you for your support: Rusty Brown, Glen Semenchuk, Pat Clayton, Hiske Gerding, Marilyn Cooke, Cheryl Hunt, Les Wetter, Margaret Green, Jan Young, Grant Nieman, Myrna Pearman, Joanne Susut, Joanne Hepburn, Carol Smith, Al Kananen, Kevin Van Tighem, Larry Simpson, Doris and Eric Hopkins, Glenn Pauley, Joel Nicolson, Brad Fenson, Andrew Schoepf, Cheryl Bradley, Glen Lawrence, Rachel Kilsdonk, Bernadette Kelly, Mary Ann McConnell-Boehm, Heather McRae, Terry Neraasen, Jacquie Gilson, Jack Sherman, Harvey Scott, Ken Gurr, Tom Cameron, Locke Girvan, Kathy Stanley, Denis and Trudy Ayotte, Doug Ringstrom, Geoff Holroyd, Dave Scobie, Lorne Fitch, Michael Prencipe, Jean Burgess, Howard Fix, Robert Kershaw, Kay Wark, Joseph Welsh School, Barry Adams, Frank Liszczak, Steve Brechtel, John Helder, Diana Keith, Howard Samoil, Peter Kilsdonk, Archie Landals, Nonie Swinnerton, Kim Lakeman, Sam Wirzba, Jamie Fortune, Janice ter Borg, and Anthony Sharp.

Special thanks to Gilda Sanders, Arlene Kwasniak and Marc Denhez for reviewing earlier drafts of this manuscript. Any shortcomings revealed in the following pages are my own.

Finally, I thank Rusty, Caitlin and Arthur for their ongoing encouragement and support.

Financial assistance for this project was generously provided by:

ACTION 21
Environment Canada
Working together for a healthier environment

FRIENDS
of the
ENVIRONMENT
Foundation

Alberta
Sport Recreation
Parks & Wildlife
Foundation

Other contributing partners include:
Alberta Conservation Association; Alberta Environmental Protection; Alberta Fish and Game Association; Alberta Land Stewards Network; Canadian Wildlife Service; City of Edmonton; Crooked Creek Conservancy of Athabasca; Ducks Unlimited Canada; Environmental Law Centre; Federation of Alberta Naturalists; Land Stewardship Centre of Canada; Red Deer River Naturalists, Rocky Mountain Elk Foundation; South Country Protected Areas Project; Southern Alberta Land Trust Society; and Nature Conservancy of Canada.

Foreword

by Kevin Van Tighem

Conservation takes place in the real world. That's what makes it so complicated.

In an idealized world, we could protect all of nature in parks and wilderness areas. We would not need to worry about growing and selling crops, ensuring the financial security of our children, or solving complicated problems about how to manage our own property. We could just enjoy unspoiled nature in a state of perpetual, worry-free bliss.

But in the real world, parks and wilderness will never amount to more than just a small portion of the living landscape. Farms, acreages, towns, managed forests, mines, and other land uses will dominate the rest. Real people, with real problems, will dwell there. And since birds and mammals, plants and streams show a notorious inability to care about the invisible lines we draw across the land, the future of nature's living diversity will always depend a lot more on the choices those real people make at home than it will on the protection of the parks we sometimes visit.

We live in troubled times. Change besets us all. Ranchers worry about whether the kids will choose to continue family traditions—or will they succumb to the temptation to subdivide the family ranch and sell it at inflated recreational real estate prices? Farmers watch as towns and cities spread closer and closer, engulfing fields that once grew wheat, canola and good neighbours. Real estate values climb beyond the reach of ordinary Albertans. New "No Trespassing" signs and stuccoed monster homes spring up daily, signaling more absentee owners of the rural landscape. Conservationists watch elk winter ranges carved up into ranchettes, productive wetlands filled in, privately owned forests clear cut.

We all spend more time worrying about the future than we used to. How can we retain the things we love about our home place, our native Alberta landscapes, when so many forces seem to be arrayed against us? How can the ordinary Albertan with a bit of land and a mortgage really hope to make a difference?

We could wake up one morning and no longer recognize what we see outside as home. Bit by bit, compromise by compromise, we could allow this place to cease to be the Alberta we know and love. It could happen in our lifetimes; it could happen very soon.

But it need not happen at all. That is Lesley Curthoys' message, and it is a message of hope and empowerment. We need not be victims of forces beyond our control. We can choose to protect the things we cherish about our home landscapes, and our own property; in doing so we can choose from a surprisingly varied assortment of legal tools and techniques. Those of us who worry about the financial costs of protecting the agricultural use of the family farm or ranch, or the conservation values of a well-loved acreage or a particularly valuable piece of wildlife habitat may actually be able to avoid those costs. In some cases, we might be able to come out ahead.

Imagine that!

Somewhere along the way, late in the twentieth century, many Albertans began to sense a loss of personal power and control. The future has increasingly ceased to be a place of hope and started to become something to fear. Conservationists, panicking over the continued loss of wild places and native wildlife, call for more parks, stricter laws, more regulation. Landowners, faced with more regulation, higher taxes, and increasingly complex land-use controls, become more and more suspicious of government and special interest groups. We all suffer from the same ailment; we just see it differently. We all fear the consequences of losing personal control over the important changes that affect our lives and our property.

Now, with voluntary private land conservancy, we have powerful new tools to control and direct change. We can ensure that the family farm continues as agricultural land. We can make sure the ranch is never broken up. We can protect wildlife and its habitat. At the same time, we can plan wisely and responsibly for the financial security of our families. And in doing so, we can bestow lasting benefits on our rural communities and our beautiful Alberta landscapes. We can leave a legacy of love and farsightedness to those who will come after us.

All Albertans owe Lesley Curthoys a debt of gratitude for assembling this book. She has given us a road map to a sustainable future in which conservationists, landowners, charitable organizations, local governments, and philanthropists can work together on behalf of the rich, living landscapes of the Alberta we all love so dearly.

Now it only remains for us to use it.

Kevin Van Tighem is a fourth-generation Albertan, conservationist, father, and author of many articles and books on wildlife and conservation. His most recent book is *Coming West: A Natural History of Home.*

Chapter 1   Visualizing a Brighter Future

Alberta is blessed with a bountiful natural legacy. Today, more than ever, the fate of that legacy lies in the hands of private citizens.

Many Albertans respect and cherish our natural heritage. Their love of Alberta is reflected by generations of sound land management and by innumerable hours volunteered to conservation projects across the province.

However, we cannot deny that, despite past and ongoing stewardship efforts, our natural legacy is disappearing at an alarming rate. A combination of complex factors is exerting tremendous pressure on our land base. The end result, as shown below, is landscape fragmentation and destruction of natural habitat.

| 1949 | 1991 |

As these two photographs of an area near Swan Hills show, our rural landscape is undergoing rapid changes: in just 42 years, this land's biodiversity has been severely depleted by intensive land use. Photo sequence compiled by Richard G. Thomas.   Photo credit: Alberta Environmental Protection- Air Photo Services, Edmonton.

Ancient forests, vast prairies, spectacular mountain meadows, rich wetlands, and free-flowing rivers are rapidly being lost to roads, parking lots, housing developments, marginal crops, clearcuts, seismic lines—the list goes on and on. Along with the loss of natural places, comes the loss of opportunities to live in harmony with the land, and even the loss of once-thriving rural communities.

A depressing picture, isn't it? I believe, as I am sure you do, that our children and grandchildren deserve a brighter future. But what does that future look like? And how do we get off our current path of "progress at all costs" and onto a more life-respecting one?

Visualization is a popular topic in human development literature. Advocates of this personal development strategy suggest that to make changes in our lives, we need to visualize those changes: to see the person we want to become; to envision the preferred outcome of an event. In doing so, we focus on the positive image, channeling our creative energies to make it a reality.

Can we not apply this same visualization process to saving our natural heritage? Rather than dwelling on negative scenarios that leave us in despair, we can envision a prosperous, healthy Alberta. Unfortunately, too many well-meaning people working to protect our future dwell on ecological disasters. I know I did. My wake-up call arrived several years ago when my four-year-old daughter expressed her fear about the world's future. Her despair shocked and saddened me, for no child should carry that burden. I realized then that it was time to change my outlook. It was time to deal with the undeniable environmental crisis in a more positive, constructive way. For the sake of my children, and all young people, it was time for me to see and believe in a brighter future.

If, as a society, we see "progress" as just more of the same—more malls, more fast-food joints, more roads, more urbanization at the expense of productive soils, more foreign control over our natural assets, and so forth—then so it shall be. Look around. It is becoming a reality in many regions of Alberta. Sadly, distinct communities—mosaics of natural, cultural, and historical values—are being replaced by the homogenized face of progress. We must ask ourselves: Does this picture reflect who we are and what we truly value? Is this the Alberta we desire?

Perhaps it is time to redefine what we mean by progress. The first step is to take careful stock of what we care about on our own land, in our communities, and in this glorious province. With this knowledge, we can work to safeguard these important values. No doubt each of us will envision a different future, but the basics will likely be the same: clean and ample water, breathable air, productive soils, local control over land-use decisions, places to relax, and protection of our sacred places. Visualizing a prosperous Alberta with its bountiful natural legacy intact is a positive way to build a future we will be proud to pass on. Saving our natural legacy is sound insurance for a secure tomorrow. And what better gift can

Rusty Brown

Lesley Curthoys

we give Alberta's young people than a secure future?

The private conservancy options described in this book provide an important way to make our common vision of a brighter future a reality. As you will see, there are a wide range of tools to choose from. Along with easy-to-read descriptions of each conservation option, you will find answers to commonly asked questions. Each chapter concludes with a list of organizations that can provide you with answers to your specific questions. Appendix A gives an overview of Alberta's conservation organizations, including contact information, while Appendix B provides a list of useful resources.

I trust this private conservancy guide helps you achieve your future vision of a vibrant Alberta landscape.

Chapter 2   Exploring Your Options

There are various ways for individuals to contribute to protecting Alberta's natural heritage. Your options will depend on whether or not you own land, on the land's conservation values, on your personal land ethic, and on your financial situation. This chapter provides a general overview of factors to consider as you explore your private conservancy options.

The decision to protect land is a serious one, worthy of careful thought. Making a sound decision involves three steps:

1. assessing your goals and needs;

2. reviewing your options; and

3. knowing who to contact for additional help or information.

Assessing Your Goals and Needs

Even if you do not own land, or if your land lacks significant natural values, you still can become involved in land-saving projects. Chapter 8 explains ways of making charitable donations to generate much-needed conservation funds.

If you do own land and cherish its natural qualities, no doubt you have concerns about its future. Landowners may wonder: "What is the best way to care for the land while maintaining existing land uses?" "Can I develop my land and still preserve its tranquillity?" "How can I ensure that future landowners will care for the land as I have?" "Will my children or others be able to enjoy its recreational opportunities and beauty?"

Addressing such concerns begins with assessing your individual financial and personal needs, and desires for the land. You should consider the factors listed below.

Ownership—Do you want to retain ownership of your land? If you decide to transfer the title, will it be through donation or sale? To whom do you want to transfer title?

Residence—Do you or your children want to continue living on the land?

Land Quality—In what ways is your land special? What features would you like to see protected? How does your land contribute to Alberta's natural heritage or your local community's well-being?

Type of Protection—What types of future land uses do you envision? Do you wish to continue traditional land-uses, allow recreational activities, or enforce strict land-use restrictions? Do you need to apply protective measures to all or just a portion of the property? Do you wish to protect your land for a limited time or forever?

Financial Situation—Can you afford to give up the developmental potential of your land? Do you need to earn an income from your land? If so, do you require financial compensation immediately or over a long period? Will the financial benefits offset the cost of putting the protective measures in place? Have you assessed the tax implications?

Family Issues—Do the members of your family share your land protection vision? What are their hopes or intentions for the property?

Reviewing Your Options

The next step in planning the future of your land is to match your needs with the most appropriate conservation option. Each person's situation will differ, and therefore each person will require different tools or combinations of tools to achieve the desired goals.

The diversity and versatility of available conservation tools allows Albertans to take a responsible and creative approach to land use. Conservation and land use can occur together, often with beneficial results. For example, Alberta ranchers who protect riparian habitats benefit from increased rangeland productivity; while vacation resort owners who protect their property's wildlife viewing opportunities have more to offer their clients.

All of the conservation options discussed in this book are voluntary. They range from informal agreements to continue caring for your land as you currently do, to formal legal mechanisms that ensure protection in perpetuity. Each option varies in its flexibility, the strength and duration of the protection it offers, its financial implications, its legal complexity, and the degree of involvement with a conservation organization that it requires. Furthermore, each technique can be tailored to meet your individual situation.

Alberta's conservation options fall into the five general categories shown below:

1. stewardship recognition programs;

2. contracts;

3. deed restrictions—conservation easements and related common law tools;

4. transfer of ownership to a land trust through sale or donation; and

5. donation of assets to generate conservation funds.

The following chart provides an overview of Alberta's private conservancy options.

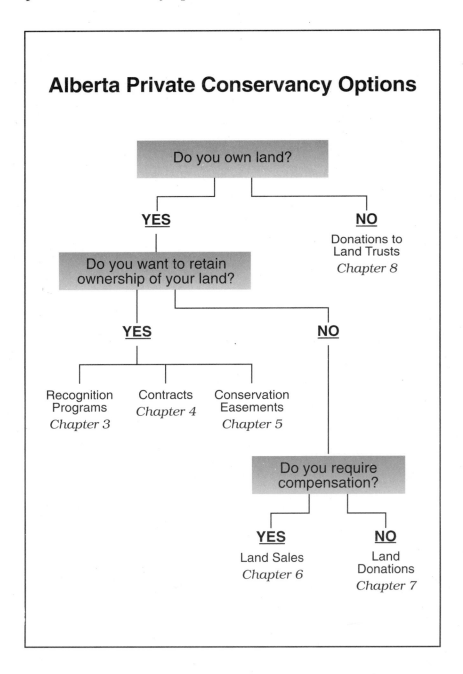

Alberta Private Conservancy Options

Do you own land?

YES

NO
Donations to
Land Trusts
Chapter 8

Do you want to retain
ownership of your land?

YES

NO

Recognition
Programs
Chapter 3

Contracts
Chapter 4

Conservation
Easements
Chapter 5

Do you require
compensation?

YES
Land Sales
Chapter 6

NO
Land
Donations
Chapter 7

Knowing Who Can Help

Often, land protection involves working with a conservation partner—a land protection agency that can offer advice and help you realize your conservation goals. In fact, some conservation options are not possible without the co-operation of an organization. In these situations, protection will only be as good as the agency entrusted with the long-term guardianship of your land's natural values. Consequently, it is important to find a conservation partner that is philosophically and fiscally committed to your land protection goals.

Some key questions to consider in your evaluation of which conservation organization best meets your needs include the following:

1. What are the organization's conservation goals and priorities?
2. Does it have the resources (staff, cash, sound history, solid future) to care for your land as you wish?
3. What type of assistance does it offer (professional advice, land stewardship assistance, ecological value assessment, or financial support)?

The organization, too, is making a major commitment of its time and money, and will therefore want to be sure that the agreement meets its mandate and is within its capacity. For example, if an organization's mandate is to protect wetlands, it may not be interested in old-growth forest, in spite of this habitat's importance for migratory song birds.

You will find a list of possible partner organizations at the end of each chapter. You can then check Appendix A, which provides a brief description of each organization as well as contact information.

High Priority Conservation Lands

Generally speaking, high priority conservation lands include sacred places; lands with species or ecosystems at risk, such as prairie plants, animals, and their native grassland habitat; lands that have a low level of disturbance; sensitive ecosystems; areas of wildlife concentration, such as elk wintering yards and heronries; places that are vital to overall landscape health, such as wetlands, riparian habitats, or river corridors; areas used by migratory birds as stopover points, feeding areas, or breeding grounds; or lands that have outstanding scenic, educational, or research values.

If the conservation option of your choice uses legal techniques and could have significant financial implications, you should seek legal and financial advice.

As is the case with most worthwhile goals, finding the right conservation option will take time and perseverance. Your decision to protect the natural features of your land, or to donate your assets to a land-saving organization, is an important one. The following chapters will help you address many of the questions this decision raises.

Chapter 3 Stewardship Recognition Programs

A commitment to protecting Alberta's natural heritage —clean air, healthy water, productive soils, beautiful vistas, wildlife habitats, and biodiversity—begins with how we care for our land and local communities. Whether we live in cities, suburbs, or rural areas, our daily actions determine the future health of this outstanding province we call home.

If you already practise responsible land stewardship, you may want to consider participating in a recognition program. If you do, you will be recognized for your commitment to Alberta's natural environment. Furthermore, your involvement will increase local awareness of ways to conserve nature, and may encourage others to follow your example. Indeed, the success of many conservation programs depends on role models within the community.

Promoting a Conservation Ethic

Land stewardship recognition programs pay tribute to landowners who conserve wildlife habitat. These programs simply involve a landowner's voluntary consent to continue practising wildlife conservation. Often, participants place a sign on their property declaring their partnership with a certain conservation program.

The general goal of a land stewardship recognition program is to say "thank you" to those who put their conservation ethic into action. Examples of responsible land stewardship practices include:

- saving wildlife habitat located on your property;
- integrating soil, water, and wildlife conservation into your normal use of land (for example, fencing cattle away from fragile riparian areas);
- refraining from disturbing nesting areas, such as those of the endangered burrowing owl; and
- planting native species that benefit wildlife.

Participating in a land stewardship recognition program is the easiest conservation option available in Alberta; yet, through its contribution to awareness and education, it can have far-reaching ripple effects by encouraging others to adopt a conservation ethic.

Common Questions

Does this conservation option affect my rights as a landowner? The landowner retains full rights to land use (as permitted by existing laws and bylaws). Essentially, you would continue to do what you have been doing through your own initiative, only now you are recognized for your efforts. Involvement in the program is ended simply by contacting the organization.

How secure is this conservation option? With this conservation option, the cherished natural values of your land will be safeguarded only as long as you are the landowner. Other options (discussed in the following chapters) provide more permanent protection.

What are the benefits? In recognition of your important contribution to protecting or enhancing wildlife habitats, the organization usually provides a certificate, wall plaque, or gate sign. Other benefits may include newsletters, and assistance with conservation projects.

What are the disadvantages? The major disadvantage of landowner recognition programs is that control is lost when the property changes hands. In other words, everything that you value and have worked to protect could be lost forever. To ensure a lasting legacy, you may wish to combine this conservation option with more permanent protective measures, such as registering a conservation easement against your land's title (Chapter 5), or selling or donating your property to a land trust (Chapters 6 and 7, respectively).

Who to Contact

If you are interested in participating in one of Alberta's land stewardship recognition programs, or would like to nominate a landowner you believe deserves recognition for voluntary stewardship efforts, you can contact either the Alberta Fish and Game Association or the Red Deer River Naturalists. For more information on these organizations, please see Appendix A. Their stewardship recognition programs are described in the following pages.

Alberta Fish and Game Association

The *Habitat Steward Program* acknowledges responsible land management practices that aid in conserving wildlife and fish habitat. Fred Fredmeyer Sr., shown here, is a proud steward of Alberta's wildlife habitats in the Peace Country region.

The *Parkland Stewardship Program* recognizes individuals who own land located approximately 48 km (30 miles) east or west of Highway 2 between Edmonton and Red Deer, and who have done an excellent job of conserving parkland habitat by integrating soil, water, and wildlife conservation as part of their farming practices. Benefits include newsletters, customized farm conservation plans, and assistance with conservation projects.

Abandoned pioneer farmsteads often become refuges for wildlife. The *Heritage Farmsteads for Wildlife* program

acknowledges the current landowner for safeguarding these important refuges. In addition, the original pioneer family is identified and honoured.

The goal of the *Operation Grassland Community* program is to increase public awareness of prairie wildlife species and their survival needs. Public awareness is increased by recognizing landowners who voluntarily agree

Operation Grassland Community

to retain habitat for endangered prairie species, including the burrowing owl and loggerhead shrike. Here, Dave Scobie presents a sign to Julius Molstan in recognition of his efforts to help save burrowing owls.

Red Deer River Naturalists

NatureScape Alberta is being developed into an Alberta-wide program by the Red Deer River Naturalists in conjunction with the Federation of Alberta Naturalists. It is based on Backyards for Wildlife, a program spearheaded by both organizations in the late 1980s. The goal of NatureScape Alberta is to promote backyard and schoolyard biodiversity. This goal will be accomplished in three ways: through the publication of a book titled *NatureScape Alberta: Caring for Wildlife Habitat at Home*; through the establishment of a certification program that recognizes schools and landowners (rural and urban) who strive to attract wildlife or maximize biodiversity in their own yards and neighbourhoods; and through the development of an education program that will encourage widespread public involvement in backyard or schoolyard habitat conservation activities.

Here, students and staff at Red Deer's Joseph Welsh School share in the labour and satisfaction of building their Environmental Outdoor Classroom.

The *Habitat Steward Program* recognizes rural landowners who voluntarily conserve wildlife habitat on their property. Any type of habitat can be protected, providing that the area reserved is a minimum of five acres.

Trudy and Denis Ayotte, shown here, believe that participating in this program and having a gate sign is a positive way to raise community aware-ness about the need to set aside land for wildlife. They hope their efforts to protect nature will en-courage others to do the same.

Chapter 4 Contracts for Conservation

Conservation contracts involve a voluntary agreement to manage your land with the needs of wildlife in mind. Typically these contracts are written rather than verbal, and they are signed by the parties involved.

A personal contract helps you to maintain your land in a certain way, or allows a conservation organization to conduct specific activities on your property. Often it involves direct or indirect economic incentives for conservation practices. A contract also offers you an opportunity to get to know a conservation organization before making any long-term commitment.

Many conservation organizations support the idea of keeping land in production, but doing so in such a way that its important natural features and ecological services remain intact. Essentially, the goal of conservation contracts is to find a win-win situation, where the landowner benefits both ecologically and economically from caring for the land, and the conservation organization gets some guarantee that the property's natural values will be protected.

In Alberta, three types of contracts are used for conservation purposes: the lease or rental agreement, the management agreement, and the land-use exchange agreement. All three contracts provide temporary protection (for the term of the contract only), and may or may not be registered at Land Titles. A registered interest is transferred with title, and notifies any potential purchaser that the use of the land is subject to an existing contract.

We will look at each of these contracts separately, and then address common questions relevant to all three types. This chapter closes with a list of Alberta organizations that use contracts in their conservation work with private landowners.

Lease Agreement

The lease is the conservation option of choice for the landowner who prefers a short-term, flexible option and who requires monetary compensation for keeping some land out of agricultural production. Sometimes a conservation organization is interested in leasing high priority wildlife habitat. Ducks Unlimited, for instance, may lease lands that provide waterfowl nesting habitat.

A land lease agreement for a parcel of land gives the tenant (the conservation organization) control over the land, subject to the conditions stated in the lease contract. The lease document should state what rights and responsibilities the landowner retains during the term of the contract, what activities may or may not occur on the land, what happens if the contract is broken by either party, when the contract starts and ends, and the rental fee. The rental fee may be the normal rate for the area, or it may be a nominal fee.

A lease automatically expires at the end of its term, although it may be terminated by notice from the landlord, or as a result of a major breach of contract.

Management Agreement

A management agreement is a written contract committing one or both parties to certain responsibilities in caring for a property. The overall goal of a management agreement is to recognize landowner conservation efforts and to provide incentives for further contributions

Ducks Unlimited

Wetlands are one of our most productive wildlife habitats. Wetlands also provide free ecological services, such as water storage and stock watering, water purification, flood control, and soil erosion prevention.

to the protection of Alberta's natural heritage.

A management agreement typically helps a conservation organization meet its objectives, while providing the landowner with assistance in wise land management. It can accommodate a variety of landowner needs, such as assistance in fencing off a fragile section of a stream to prevent overgrazing and erosion problems. Other examples of management agreements include granting permission to a conservation organization to build a water control structure, agreeing to delay haying times so that ground-nesting birds have a chance to fledge, agreeing to use a flushing bar, implementing a conservation grazing system, or retaining a woodland in its natural state.

In return for entering into a management agreement, a landowner may receive one or more benefits, including a one-time recognition payment, capital improvements, or free technical advice.

A management agreement automatically expires at the end of its term, or earlier as a result of a substantial breach of contract, if the innocent party wants the contract to end. Ideally, the landowner will maintain wildlife habitat whether or not the contract is renewed.

Alberta Story

The Kelly farm, northeast of Entwistle, borders the Pembina River. For two generations, the Kellys have farmed their land while maintaining homes for wildlife. In 1996, Bernadette Kelly and Jesse Kelly entered into a "Buck for Wildlife" habitat retention agreement with Alberta Environmental Protection to continue protecting wildlife habitat. Essentially this conservation contract was an agreement to continue farming as usual, with the added bonus of a one-time recognition payment for their commitment to conservation.

Lesley Curthoys

The ten-year contract stipulates that the woodland and wetland habitats (called the habitat lands) would not be reduced or destroyed. A beautiful old-growth white spruce forest—considered sacred by Bernadette, as it was by her grandfather—will remain untouched, while grazing and haying operations continue as before. Incidental grazing and building of a small cabin on the habitat lands are permitted, so long as these activities do not diminish the conservation value of these lands.

Most lands to the south and east of the Pembina River have been denuded of forests. What sparse woodland habitat remains is now under threat of clearance by logging companies seeking timber on private lands. The wisdom and commitment of landowners like the Kelly family, provide hope that some private forested areas will remain alive and thriving, and will continue to provide vital riverside habitat.

Alberta Story

Parkland habitat is characterized by a gently rolling tapestry of woodlands, grasslands, shrublands, and pothole sloughs. This diverse natural mosaic makes  Alberta's parklands one of the most significant bird breeding areas in North America. In fact, some refer to it as North America's "duck factory." Less than 13% of the world's parkland habitat remains. Glen Lawrence's home quarter contributes to that 13%.

Glen is a fourth-generation farmer and a building contractor who specializes in energy efficient designs. In keeping with his belief that a better future begins with individual action, he bought a quarter section of land with the intention of keeping it natural, built a home that places minimal demands on the land, and successfully farms other properties without the use of any chemicals.

Some people think of land allowed to remain natural as "idle" or even "wasteful." Not Glen. He recognizes that his quarter is far from idle: every hour it is producing clean air, recharging water sources, making soil, acting as a windbreak, providing homes for wildlife, and overall, contributing to the rural landscape's beauty.

When asked by Ducks Unlimited to participate in its Cooking Lake Moraine Pilot Project (established to conserve and enhance important duck breeding areas in the region) Glen was happy to co-operate. He signed a ten-year conservation agreement to maintain 150 acres of his property in its existing natural state. Ducks Unlimited has been given permission to access the land to install nesting structures. This agreement will not interfere with Glen's future plans to use more permanent private conservancy tools.

Land-use Exchange

Ducks Unlimited Canada offers a third type of conservation contract—the land-use exchange. With this personal contract, an agricultural producer agrees to conserve habitat areas in return for use of productive agricultural land owned by Ducks Unlimited. Generally, the habitat areas have a lower agricultural value, or are too wet to farm, making this agreement a win-win situation for agricultural producers, wildlife agencies, and of course, wildlife species dependent on wetland and upland habitats.

Common Questions

Does a contract affect my rights and responsibilities as a landowner? With all three types of personal contracts, the landowner retains title to the land. The specific covenants (promises) of the agreement are negotiated between the landowner and the organization. The landowner retains the responsibility of ensuring that land uses abide by existing laws, and he or she remains responsible for property taxes. Also, under the Alberta *Occupiers' Liability Act*, both parties to the agreement could be held responsible if someone is injured on the property.

How is a contract ended?	A personal contract expires automatically at the end of the contract term, or sooner if there is a substantial breach of contract or if the parties to the agreement cease to exist. Contracts may have a payout option.
How secure is this conservation option?	The conditions of the agreement are enforceable by law, but only for the term of the contract, and only between the parties to the agreement. Under the *Land Titles Act*, if the lease is for three years or less, it will bind future purchasers. If the lease is for more than three years, then it must be registered to bind future owners.
What happens if the contract is broken by either party?	The consequences of breaking a contract will vary depending on the terms of the contract or the ruling by a court of law. The contract will set out what enforcement mechanisms are available if there is a breach of contract. As with any important agreement, it is wise to ensure that you clearly understand your obligations as well as those of the other party, and that you know what actions can be taken if the agreement is violated.
What are the benefits?	A personal contract is a flexible conservation option. The specific uses of the land and the duration of the contract are negotiated between the landowner and the conservation organization. This conservation option usually allows for multiple use, and therefore is acceptable to landowners

who wish to combine conservation with other land uses. Conservation agreements may provide monetary compensation, such as rental payments or a one-time recognition payment, which can help offset the landowner's costs in maintaining the property. Some contracts provide indirect economic benefits through provision of seed, fence materials, or water storage facilities. In some cases, the landowner owns the improvements made to the land. A third benefit is the educational component of contracts; that is, free advice about conservation techniques.

What are the disadvantages? A disadvantage of the contract as a conservation tool, both for the land-owner and the conservation organization, is its insecurity. The conditions of the contract are only enforceable during the contract term and between contracting parties. Also, obligations to care for the natural features of the land may not be transferred with changes in ownership. The conservation easement (Chapter 5) is the preferred conservation option if you seek long-term, secure land protection.

Who to Contact

Each of the organizations listed below uses personal contracts as one of its conservation options. Sample copies of personal contracts may be available on request. For more information, please see Appendix A.

- Alberta Conservation Association
- Ducks Unlimited Canada

Chapter 5   Conservation Easements

Chapter 5 presents Alberta's newest and strongest private conservancy tool: the conservation easement. Conservation easements became a reality in Alberta in the fall of 1996 when the provincial government amended the *Environmental Protection and Enhancement Act* (EPEA). The Environmental Law Centre guided this important law reform, with support from many individuals, conservation organizations, and government agencies.

The following information provides a general introduction to conservation easements: how they work, their advantages and disadvantages as a land protection tool, and some of their tax implications. A more comprehensive review, including related legal processes and tax benefits, is found in Arlene Kwasniak's publication, *Conservation Easement Guide for Alberta*, available from the Environmental Law Centre.

A conservation easement is a voluntary legal agreement between a landowner and a qualified organization. Under its provisions, any registered landowner— whether a private citizen, corporation, or government—is able to retain ownership of land while transferring specific use rights to a qualified organization. These rights are granted for the purpose of protecting natural values on a long-term or permanent basis, and are decided on by the parties to the agreement.

The easement-holding organization has the power to monitor and enforce the conditions of the agreement. A registered conservation easement ensures that all present and future owners are bound by the conditions of the agreement, either for a specific number of years or forever.

Alberta Story

Carol Smith loves her land, with its hayfields, wooded ponds, and abundant wildlife. She also firmly believes that responsible land stewardship begins with the owner. Carol's dream was to protect—forever—the wildlife habi-

Howard Fix

tat on her land. However, Carol had to put this dream on hold because adequate legislation did not exist.

Motivated by her commitment to the natural world, her concern for future generations, and her belief in private land conservation, Carol lobbied for legislative changes. When an amendment to the *Environmental Protection and Enhancement Act* created conservation easements in Alberta, Carol finally had the legislative tool she needed to make her long-time dream a reality.

In 1997, Carol placed a conservation easement on 80

acres of her property, retaining the remaining 80 acres for its traditional livestock grazing use. Her conservation strategy also includes plans to develop hiking and cross-country ski trails. The conservation easement is held by Alberta Environmental Protection (Fish and Wildlife).

In Carol's words, "Why did I negotiate a conservation easement on the property? To show that dreams can come true. To demonstrate that with perseverance and determination even the Alberta government can be moved to do something beneficial for the natural environment. To conserve a small piece of the natural environment for all the living creatures great and small that I share it with. For all of the above."

Private property owners can voluntarily donate or sell conservation easements to a conservation organization, such as a land trust, and still retain ownership of their property.

Another way to use a conservation easement to achieve long-term protection goals is to grant a conservation easement prior to transferring title of the property. The conservation easement will bind all future landowners to use the land as stated in the conservation easement agreement. In this way, the landowner can enjoy the financial gains of transferring land, and have the peace of mind of knowing that the land will be cared for in generations to come.

Common Questions

Does a conservation easement affect my rights and responsibilities as a landowner? If the landowner decides to retain title to his or her land, then he or she retains all the use rights, except those that have been voluntarily granted to the easement-holding organization. For example, with a conservation easement established to protect wetlands, the landowner might not be allowed to apply to a government agency to drain wetlands within the conservation easement area. The owner continues to control public access, unless a different arrangement has been agreed to by the landowner and easement holder. The landowner retains responsibility for payment of property taxes, and responsibility for land maintenance as required by municipal bylaws. Under the Alberta *Occupiers' Liability Act*, both the landowner and the qualified organization holding the conservation easement could be held responsible if someone is injured on land covered by the conservation easement.

How secure is this conservation option? The conservation easement offers the greatest security in long-term land protection of all the options discussed in this guide. A conservation easement made in perpetuity provides a "permanent" form of protection—as permanent as possible, that is, within our land laws, under which the Crown is defined as the ultimate owner of most lands, and thus retains expropriation rights. As discussed later, there are three ways that a conservation easement can be modified or terminated.

A properly registered conservation easement will be transferred with the land, and it therefore binds all future landowners to the conditions of the agreement. Lasting protection requires that someone takes responsibility for ensuring that the restrictions are honoured, and that the land is being cared for as originally intended. With conservation easements, this important responsibility belongs to the easement-holding organization. If the original organization should no longer be able to hold the conservation easement, it can be assigned to another qualified organization. If the easement-holding organization dissolves, then the easement must be assigned to another qualified organization.

How does a mortgage affect a conservation easement?

The legislation governing Alberta Land Titles is based on a priority system, in which the date of registration determines which interests have priority. If a mortgage is registered before the conservation easement, then foreclosure may extinguish the conservation easement. To avoid this possibility, the landowner may approach the mortgagee for "postponement of interest" which, once registered on title, gives the conservation easement priority over the mortgage. If the easement is registered before the mortgage, it has priority, and so would survive foreclosure.

How do I enter into a conservation easement agreement?

To create a conservation easement, the first step is to determine what you want to protect and for how long. With the needs of your land in mind, you can then select the most appropriate qualified organization. Chapter 2 provides an overview of what to consider in choosing an organization. In addition, provisions of the *Environmental Protection and Enhancement Act* must be complied with to create a valid, binding conservation easement. These provisions are described below.

• Authorized Purposes
As stated in the Alberta *Environmental Protection and Enhancement Act* (S.A. 1992, c. E-13), the authorized purposes of a conservation easement are

"(a) the protection, conservation and enhancement of the environment including, without limitation, the protection, conservation, and enhancement of biological diversity;

(b) the protection, conservation and enhancement of natural scenic or aesthetic values;

(c) providing for any or all of the following uses of land that are consistent with purposes set out in clause (a) or (b):

   (i)   recreational use;

   (ii) open space use;

   (iii) environmental education use;

   (iv) use for research and scientific studies of natural ecosystems."

• Qualified Organization
The holder of the easement (or grantee) must be a "qualified organization," defined by the Act as any level of government; or a nongovernment, nonprofit organization that is registered under the Alberta *Societies Act*, has charitable status with Revenue

Canada, has objectives which include the holding of land or interests in land, and has stated in its constitution the obligation to transfer all conservation easements to another qualified organization upon winding up its operations.

• Registration
The conservation easement and any subsequent modifications to the agreement must be registered on title at the appropriate Land Titles Office.

• Notification
A 60-day notice of intention to register a conservation easement must be given to (1) the Minister of Municipal Affairs, if the land is located in an improvement district, (2) the Special Areas Board, if the land is located in a special area, and (3) the local authority of the municipality where the land is located, unless the conservation easement is being granted to that local authority. Note that the Act only gives these government bodies the right to be notified; it does not give them the right to challenge or prohibit the granting of the conservation easement. The notice period may be shortened by the person or body entitled to receive notice.

Can a conservation easement be modified or terminated? Yes. There are three ways to modify or terminate a conservation easement. The first way is by agreement of the landowner who granted the easement (grantor) and the easement holder (grantee). The second way is by order of the Minister of Environmental Protection in the public interest. A third method is by a court order that proves that the modification is beneficial to those people principally interested in the conservation easement's enforcement, or that the conservation easement directly conflicts with a land-use bylaw or statutory plan under Part 17 of the *Municipal Government Act*. For example, a conservation easement agreement could not be defeated if it were more restrictive than a land-use bylaw or statutory plan. All changes to the conservation easement agreement must be registered at the appropriate Land Titles Office.

What are the benefits? In addition to the conservation easement's security in land protection, landowners also will appreciate the flexibility of this private conservancy tool. Each conservation easement will be unique, because each is designed to reflect the landowner's individual needs, the land's natural assets, and the easement-holding organization's conservation priorities. The specific terms of the easement are negotiated between the landowner and the holder of the easement. Protection can range from no use (leaving the land in its natural state) to multiple use (allowing agricultural, recreational, and other uses that do not interfere with the purposes authorized by the Act and the specific purposes stated in the conservation easement agreement). A conservation easement can restrict land uses (such as intensive grazing, forest clearing or wetland drainage), or it can place obligations on the landowner to do certain things (such as maintain a weir or fence-off a fragile riparian area). Furthermore, conservation easements can be placed on all or on just a portion of the property. For example, the easement could be placed on the riparian areas of a ranching operation, the nesting grounds of a burrowing owl colony, or even on a patch of rare orchids. Lastly, donating a conservation easement to a qualified recipient may result in income tax benefits.

What are the disadvantages? A conservation easement may reduce property value, especially if it limits the development potential of the land. Consequently, if the property is your primary investment, you will want to have an experienced land appraiser determine the effect of granting a conservation easement. Another disadvantage of the conservation easement as a private conservancy tool is its legal complexity. The conservation easement document, with pages of legal language, may be overwhelming; however, this degree of detail is essential to give the agreement enduring legal strength. Although the landowner will be working with a qualified organization to draft this document, it may be necessary to obtain independent professional advice from land appraisers, accountants and lawyers, and possibly to contract the services of an Alberta land surveyor if required by the Land Titles Office.

Payment of these expenses is negotiated between the parties to the agreement. The legal complexity of a conservation easement also requires that landowners allow ample time for the completion of the necessary steps.

What are the property tax implications of granting a conservation easement?

Property tax implications are uncertain, as granting a conservation easement may result in an increase, decrease, or no change in property taxes. Changes to property classification and assessment value that result from granting a conservation easement determine subsequent property taxation. Because each taxation situation is different, it is wise to consult with your taxing authority to determine how property taxes will be affected, before granting a conservation easement.

What are the income tax implications of selling or donating a conservation easement?

Specific calculations of income tax implications are complex and require professional advice from an accountant or tax specialist. The following general statements are based on federal budget measures announced February 18, 1997. Land (including covenants and easements) is considered to be capital property by Revenue Canada. Consequently, when land is transferred, either by donation or sale, Revenue Canada considers that the property has been disposed of, and therefore the landowner is obligated to report any capital gain (or loss) on his or her income tax return. Any capital gain that the owner has made on the property since acquiring it may be subject to tax.

Seventy-five percent of any capital gain must be reported as income for the year of disposition. As shown in the example below, the tax credit (or deduction, in the case of corporations) may offset the tax on the capital gain. Also, a capital gains reduction is available for qualified farm property. When transferring a conservation easement, the capital gain (or loss) is calculated by subtracting the adjusted cost base (ACB) from the proceeds of disposition (the selling price) or the deemed proceeds of disposition (the value of the conservation easement at the time it was donated). However, it should be noted that calculating the conservation easement's ACB is a difficult task. The reason for this difficulty is that the conservation easement was never "acquired," rather it was "carved out" of the landowner's existing property rights. Consequently, the ACB should be calculated by an appraiser according to methods acceptable to Revenue Canada.

The tax credit or deduction is limited to 75% of your net income for the year that the donation was made. However, the total eligible claim does not have to be used in the year the donation was given. Any unused portion of your donation can be carried over for up to five years. If the conservation easement qualifies as ecologically significant land and it is donated to a qualified recipient (see the list below), the income limitation is increased to 100%.

Theoretical Example: Conservation Easement Donation

In 1997, a landowner donated a conservation easement with a fair market value (FMV) of $125,000. If the ACB of the easement is $25,000, then the capital gain resulting from the disposition of this capital property is $100,000.

Assuming the donor's income is $60,000 and no capital gains deductions were made, the donor's allowable deduction limit would be $138,750. This deduction can be used to eliminate the taxable gain ($75,000), leaving $63,750 to offset future income for up to five years.

Donor's 1997 Total Income is $135,000

Regular Income plus	$ 60,000
Taxable Capital Gain [.75 x (FMV - ACB)]	$ 75,000
	$135,000

Total allowable deduction limit is $138,750

75% of income* plus	$101,250
50% of taxable capital gain	$ 37,500
	$138,750

*This is the proposed donation limit established in the 1997 Federal Budget. The deduction limit is increased to 100% of income for gifts of ecologically sensitive lands.

Adapted from Kwasniak, Arlene J. 1997. *Conservation Easement Guide for Alberta.* Environmental Law Centre, Edmonton, Alberta. page 42

Alberta Story

For more than three generations, the Pharis family has run the Elkhorn Ranch, located on the eastern slopes of the Rockies, 30 km north of Lundbreck. Three flowing creeks and lush natural meadows surrounded by mature forests make Elkhorn Ranch prime cattle rangeland. The ranch also provides excellent wildlife habitat, including elk calving grounds.

Alta and Hilton Pharis have long recognized the special natural features of their land. They believe that sound land stewardship that maintains the health of streams, native grassland, and forest goes hand-in-hand with a viable commercial ranch. For example, Hilton and Alta, as well as many of their neighbours, are co-operators with the "Cows and Fish Project" (formerly known as the Alberta Riparian Habitat Management Project).

With intensive logging and subdivision pressures increasing, Hilton and Alta worried about the future of the valley and their home.

Working together with the Nature Conservancy of Canada, the Pharis family secured the long-term protection of Elkhorn Ranch with a conservation easement. Other conservation partners include the Alberta Fish and Game Association, the Rocky Mountain Elk Foundation, and Alberta Environmental Protection. The conservation easement agreement (held by the Nature Conservancy of Canada) prohibits future subdivision and road construction on 1700 acres.

Although they stood to make a substantial financial

gain by subdividing and selling the deeded portion of their 6500-acre ranch operation, Alta and Hilton Pharis chose to safeguard their priceless legacy by using a conservation easement.

Related Common Law Tools

A restrictive covenant is a common law tool that can be used to protect land in perpetuity or for a specified period of time. It is an agreement between landowners of nearby properties, where one landowner agrees *not* to do something on his or her property, for the benefit of the other person's property. To be valid and enforceable, the agreement must be negative in nature, and it must be shown that the one property (the dominant tenement) clearly benefits from the restrictions placed on the other property (the servient tenement). The same person may own both the restricted and benefited parcels of land.

Although cumbersome, a restrictive covenant can be a useful conservation option. Take for instance a case where neighbouring landowners share a common interest in conserving an endangered cottonwood forest that stretches along their properties. To achieve their common goal, the neighbours could use mutual restrictive covenants on each others properties to prohibit specific forest uses, such as tree cutting or cattle grazing. The covenants would be enforceable and modifiable by all parties to the agreement.

Alberta Story

In 1992, Locke Girvan and Kathy Stanley subdivided their 70 acre property into two parcels. With the co-operation of Strathcona County and the Fish and Wildlife Division of Alberta Forestry, Lands and Wildlife, Locke and Kathy used a restrictive covenant to protect 17 acres of sensitive wetland habitat along Antler Lake. The restrictive covenant was signed with the Province of Alberta. Five years later the Girvan family sold the two properties. Both parcels sold in less than one month at a prices slightly above the average market value.

Another common law tool that can be used for conservation purposes is an easement (not to be confused with the conservation easement). An easement is an agreement that permits a landowner to use the property of another owner for a specific purpose. As in the case of the restrictive covenant, one property must be benefited by the easement, otherwise the agreement is considered to be a personal contract. Also, as in a restrictive covenant, the same person may own both parcels of land.

One possible use of an easement as a conservation tool is to permit a land trust to gain access to a neighbouring property for the purpose of monitoring an important nesting area.

Neither the easement or the restrictive covenant were originally established for conservation purposes; hence, they have weaknesses that make them less than satisfactory as private conservancy tools. For example, although both run with the land and can bind subsequent owners in perpetuity, enforceability is tenuous because neither has been proven valid by Alberta courts.

Who to Contact

The organizations listed below can enter into a conservation easement agreement. For more information about these organizations, please see Appendix A.

- Alberta Conservation Association*
- Alberta Environmental Protection; contact your local Natural Resources Service office
- Alberta Fish and Game Association*
- Alberta Sport, Recreation, Parks and Wildlife Foundation*
- Ducks Unlimited Canada*
- Local authority of the municipality where the land is located*
- Nature Conservancy of Canada*
- Rocky Mountain Elk Foundation*
- Southern Alberta Land Trust Society
- Trans Canada Trail Foundation

* Denotes an organization believed to meet the criteria as a suitable recipient of ecologically sensitive lands or denotes an organization that provides assistance in pursuing a donation of ecologically sensitive lands. Contact the Canadian Wildlife Service, Environment Canada, for new listings and for more information on ecological gifts.

For more information on the legal aspects of conservation easements, restrictive covenants, or easements, contact the Environmental Law Centre.

Chapter 6   Selling Land for Conservation Purposes

In the last three chapters, we looked at conservation options available to landowners who want to retain ownership of their land. In this chapter and the following one, we discuss the conservation options open to landowners who wish to transfer ownership of their property.

You may be interested in selling your land, but may also worry that future owners will not care for its natural values as you have. Your worries are well founded, for if you do not take protective actions before you sell, your land's beauty, tranquillity, and wildlife inhabitants may very well disappear under future land uses.

To ensure continued good stewardship of your land, you can sell it to a land trust. A land trust (or conservancy, as it is sometimes called) is a nonprofit conservation organization set up to protect land for scenic, agricultural, recreational, or other conservation purposes. Also, provincial government agencies and municipalities might purchase private property important to the protection of existing public conservation lands. Alternatively, you may find that the new owners are conservation-minded and wish to carry on your land stewardship practices.

Charlie Ellis, along with his sister Winnie, operated one of the largest bluebird trails in Alberta, fed the birds each winter, planted wildlife-attracting vegetation around their

Myrna Pearman

farm, and built several dams to create wetland habitats. When Union Carbide Canada offered to purchase the

Myrna Pearman

Ellis farm, located southeast of Lacombe, Charlie and Winnie agreed to sell on condition that the company continue their bluebird conservation work. Union Carbide agreed that the Ellis legacy should continue, so they established a nonprofit, arms-length company called the Ellis Bird Farm Ltd. (EBF). The EBF's mandate is fourfold: (1) to operate a bluebird nesting program; (2) to carry out an extensive bird feeding program; (3) to undertake scientific research; and (4) to develop and deliver education programs.

The homesite section, deemed Preserve Land, continues to raise cattle, crops, and bluebirds, and will never be subject to industrial development. The original farm site is now being set up as a demonstration backyard wildlife habitat area with water gardens, butterfly gardens, hummingbird gardens, and an arboretum of wildlife-attracting trees and shrubs. The site, which has wheelchair-accessible trails, a visitor centre, and a tea house, is open to the public between June first and the Labour Day weekend.

What if you cannot find a conservation organization that meets your needs and expectations? Conversely, what if you cannot find one that wants to purchase your land? Or, what if you prefer to sell your land on the open market? In all of these situations, you can still protect the natural qualities of your land by granting a conservation easement to a qualified conservation organization prior to the sale. As noted in Chapter 5, a properly registered conservation easement will protect land after it is sold by legally binding all future landowners to respect the stewardship obligations stated in the conservation easement agreement. By granting a conservation easement, however, you may reduce the property's fair market value.

Selling Property to a Land Trust

Land trusts usually have limited funds for land purchases. Furthermore, land stewardship costs do not stop with the purchase, as there are many expenses associated with long-term care. In addition to land-care costs, the land trust is responsible for paying property taxes and public liability insurance on all its properties. As you can image, these expenses add up quickly. Ideally, a land trust should have an endowment fund for each nature sanctuary it owns. For all of the above reasons, a land trust usually buys only high priority sites (as judged by the organization's mandate and the property's degree of risk).

In some situations, it may be necessary for a land trust to run a fundraising campaign, either alone or in co-operation with other conservation groups, to secure land acquisition funds. Consequently, landowners should allow ample time to complete the land transaction.

If your property ranks low in ecological value but high in market value (such as residential housing or commercial property) you could sell it as trade land. Trade land is sold to a land trust with the understanding that the organization will sell the property and use the proceeds to build a fund for its land-saving actions and other vital land-stewardship functions, such as research and public education. In Chapter 8, we look at trade lands as well as other ways that Albertans can help build much-needed conservation funds.

Ways of Selling Land

You and the land trust can create a tailor-made land transaction deal by choosing from a variety of legal alternatives. The best alternative, or combination of alternatives, will depend on your financial needs and the preferences of the land trust interested in purchasing your property. The possibilities include:

- **outright sale**—the direct transfer of property at fair market value.

- **bargain sale**—the transfer of property at less than fair market value.

- **installment sale**—a transfer of property with payments made over a specified period of time rather than in one payment. With this type of sale, any taxes on capital gain are spread out over several years.

- **sale with a life estate**—a transfer of property where the seller retains an interest, which allows use of the property for the remainder of his or her life. This interest, called a "life estate," may be extended to named individuals. The buyer and seller agree on the responsibilities of both parties during the life estate. Both parties should obtain public liability insurance.

- **sale with a leaseback agreement**—a land transaction that involves leasing the property back to the original owner. Sometimes deed restrictions are placed on the title before the property is leased.

- **option to purchase**—an agreement that gives a potential buyer (the land trust) a specified time to raise a set sale price. A landowner may give or sell an option to purchase to the land trust. During the option period, the land cannot be sold to other buyers. The agreement does not obligate the organization to purchase the land. It should not be confused with an "offer" to purchase. An offer to purchase requires a down payment, and it legally binds the prospective buyer who signed the agreement to purchase land at the stated price by the agreed purchase date, unless released by an escape clause.

- **right of first refusal**—a legally binding agreement that gives an organization the first chance to purchase the property, should you decide to sell to a specific willing purchaser. Such an arrangement is useful when you have a specific land trust in mind, but are not certain if and when you want to sell your land. The agreement does not obligate the land trust to purchase the land.

The above legal agreements can be used in any combination, giving the landowner with heritage conservation in mind a wide variety of ways to sell land.

Blaine Marr, a rancher in southern Alberta, sold a quarter section of important wildlife habitat to the Rocky Mountain Elk Foundation with a leaseback agreement. Using this conservation option, Mr. Marr benefited financially from the proceeds of sale without sacrificing any

pasturage for his cows. The wildlife benefited too, through permanent protection of the land base. This 65 hectares of steep, rocky grasslands, called Blind Canyon, provides important rutting and lambing habitat for bighorn sheep. As buffer land adjacent to Waterton Lakes National Park, it helps sustain healthy populations of elk, deer, cougars, and grizzlies. Blind Canyon is home to rare plants, such as the Mountain Thistle and Prairie Lungwort.

Other partners in this successful conservation project are the Alberta Fish and Game Association, the Foundation for North American Wild Sheep, The Nature Conservancy of Canada, and the Alberta Ministry of Environmental Protection.

Common Questions

How secure is this conservation option? The security of selling your land to a land trust or government agency is dependent on the organization's long-term stability, resources, and commitment to conservation. As discussed in Chapter 5, you can increase the protection by placing a conservation easement on title before selling the property.

What are the benefits? One benefit of selling land to a conservation organization is the satisfaction of selling the land to an organization that will realize your land protection goals. Financial advantages include the proceeds of the sale, and the avoidance of expenses that would be involved in a realtor sale. Furthermore, in most cases, public liability insurance, property taxes, and land maintenance costs will be assumed by the new owner.

What are the disadvantages? Disadvantages include the loss of rights associated with land ownership, and the necessity of paying tax on capital gains (if any). Also, land transactions requiring subdivision can be difficult and expensive.

What are the income tax implications of selling land to a land trust? Land is considered to be capital property by Revenue Canada. When selling capital property, any capital gain or loss associated with the proceeds of disposition must be stated, and capital gains (if any) may be subject to tax. Seventy-five percent of the capital gain must be reported as income for the year of disposition. Depending on the type of legal agreement used, capital gains tax can be reduced. For example, in a bargain sale, the proceeds of disposition will be less than in an outright sale. In an installment sale, the capital gains tax can be spread out over time. If the land is considered to be "qualified farm property" by Revenue Canada, then the taxable gain would be reduced by the allowable capital gains deduction (75% of $500,000).

Who to Contact

The organizations listed below may purchase land for conservation purposes. For more information about these organizations, please see Appendix A.

- Alberta Conservation Association
- Alberta Fish and Game Association
- Alberta Sport, Recreation, Parks and Wildlife Foundation
- Crooked Creek Conservancy Society of Athabasca
- Ducks Unlimited Canada
- Nature Conservancy of Canada
- Rocky Mountain Elk Foundation
- Southern Alberta Land Trust Society

Chapter 7   Donating Land for Conservation Purposes

One of the most generous ways to contribute to Alberta's natural legacy is through a gift of land. Donating land to a secure and dedicated conservation organization is one way to ensure long-term protection after transferring title. In addition, this conservation option can result in tax benefits for the donor, if the donation qualifies as a gift under Revenue Canada guidelines, and if given to a registered charity or other qualified recipient.

Government authorities can accept private land donations for conservation purposes. Indeed, many protected areas—places of provincial pride—exist today because of the generosity of private landowners. One example is the Midland Provincial Park, donated by the McMullen family in 1979. Today, this 599 hectare cultural and natural heritage park is the site of the world-famous Royal Tyrrell Museum of Paleontology.

And of course there are many examples of private land donations given to land trusts (nonprofit conservation organizations set up to protect land for conservation purposes). These nature sanctuaries may or may not be open to the public, depending on the donor's wishes.

These gifts of private property pay tribute to the long-standing Alberta tradition of caring for the land.

As in the case of land sales, land-owners have the option of transferring all or just some of their interests in land. In the first case (land title donation), the owner transfers title to the organization entrusted with long-term care of the property. In the second situation, the owner retains ownership while donating a partial interest, such as a conservation ease-

Lesley Curthoys

ment or restrictive covenant. This chapter focuses on the first case. Chapter 5 comments on gifts of lesser interests in land.

Accepting a land donation is a time-consuming and expensive responsibility. In addition to land acquisition expenses, there are many costs associated with long-term stewardship of each property acquired. Consequently, conservation organizations often work in partnership to acquire and protect important natural areas. For example, the recipient organization may accept a land donation, and then use a management agreement to contract with someone else to manage the land. Working together is especially important when protecting large areas, such as watersheds or natural wildlife corridors, that involve a complex pattern of private and public land ownership.

Type of Land Donated

Any type of natural land can be donated, providing that the recipient agency accepts the gift.

Some land trusts will accept trade land—property low in ecological value, but high in market value. The gift is accepted, with the donor agreeing that the organization may sell the property, and use the proceeds to build a conservation fund for its land-saving actions and other vital land stewardship functions, such as research and public education. In Chapter 8 we examine other ways that Albertans can help build conservation funds.

Ecological Gifts

As part of national efforts to conserve biodiversity, the Government of Canada recently created a new charitable donation category for ecologically sensitive lands. To be eligible, ecological gifts must be certified by the Minister of the Environment as important to preserving Canada's environmental heritage. In addition, the recipient agency must be a Canadian municipality or a registered charity designated by the Minister of Environment (see the list at the end of this chapter). As discussed below, qualified ecological gifts receive special tax treatment.

Ways of Donating Land

You and the recipient organization can create a tailor-made land transaction by choosing from a variety of legal alternatives. The best alternative, or combination of alternatives, will depend on your situation, and what options are offered by the recipient organization. The possibilities include:

- **outright donation**—a voluntary transfer of title from the owner to the recipient organization during the owner's lifetime. It requires approval from the recipient organization, and signing of the deed to transfer title. The benefits of an outright donation include enjoying immediate tax advantages and avoiding complications that can arise in settling an estate.

Alberta Story

Through a generous donation of land to the Sport Recreation, Parks and Wildlife Foundation, Kathleen and Robert Wark helped establish Peaceful Valley—Alberta's first park for the elderly handicapped. The land, located in the Pigeon Lake area, overlooks the scenic Battle River.

It was Robert and Kathleen's wish that patients of

Kay Wark, Alberta Sport, Recreation and Wildlife Foundation

lodges, nursing homes, and auxiliary hospitals be able to use their land and enjoy its soothing tranquillity.

In addition to donating land, the Warks bequeathed financial support to create an endowment fund called The Peaceful Valley Trust. This fund is used to support long-term maintenance of the park, as well as to build and maintain the Peaceful Valley Day Lodge, the network of wheelchair accessible trails, and other structures that contribute to a comfortable outing. Many other donors have given generously to the trust.

- **donation by will** (also called a bequest)—a donation that becomes effective only upon death of the donor. In the will, the donor states his or her intent to transfer a land title to a specific conservation organization. It is advisable to contact the potential recipient before the will is drawn up, to ensure that the organization can accept the gift of land, and to clarify the terms of the bequest. Accepting land donated by will is a delicate matter for a land trust. Consequently, a land trust is much more willing to accept a bequest that will be supported, rather than challenged, by your heirs. Accordingly, it is advisable to discuss your intentions with your family, so that they understand your wishes and also see how the donation benefits your estate. Finally, it is advisable to identify an alternative recipient in the will, in case the original conservation organization is unable to accept the gift.

  Bequests can generate a substantial tax credit, enabling you to give more to your beneficiaries. The tax limits for gifts made in the year of death and in the immediate taxation year is 100% of the individual's net income for those years. Any unused credit may also be carried back one year.

- **donation with a life estate**—a transfer of property where the donor retains an interest which allows use of the property for the remainder of his or her life. This interest, called a "life estate," may be extended to named individuals. The advantage of this type of donation is that the donor receives a charitable donation receipt now, and still retains the right to use the property in accordance with the agreed upon conservation objectives. The tax receipt, however, will be less than that for an outright donation, because it is reduced by the value of the life interest of the landowner, based on Revenue Canada's actuarial tables.

The donor and recipient agree on the responsibilities of both parties during the life estate. Both parties should obtain public liability insurance.

Alberta Story

After a long search for a place in the country, Doris and Eric Hopkins found their beloved Coyote Lake and bought two quarters on its north shore. Their original plan was simply to retire; however, once Doris and Eric became better acquainted with the area, they realized that Coyote Lake was a wilderness gem—one of the last

Howard Fix

pristine lakes in the greater Edmonton area. They also knew that it was up to them to ensure that it continued to be a wilderness gem! This realization set in motion a rewarding twenty-year journey, not only to protect their property, but also to enclose all of Coyote Lake with protected land.

Doris and Eric firmly believe that wildlife habitat protection requires setting aside large chunks of land. To conserve "large chunks," it is necessary to share your vision, and to work with others. This is exactly what Doris and Eric did. They shared their vision to keep Coyote Lake pristine by extending a hearty welcome to visitors. Youth are especially welcome, because as Doris put it, "Young people need to have exposure to nature if they are to appreciate it, get to know it, and feel at home in it." Also, Doris and Eric have worked with many individuals to make their vision a reality. Family, friends and neighbours, the County of Leduc, the Provincial Government, and the Nature Conservancy of Canada, all played a role. Thanks to the efforts of the Natural Areas staff, a crown section on the lake was designated as a Natural Area. When the Nature Conservancy learned that Coyote Lake had been designated an ecologically significant area by the County of Leduc and the provincial government, it purchased two privately owned lake-shore quarter sections. The Hopkins then donated their land to the Nature Conservancy, and the 960 acre Coyote Lake Conservation Area came into being. Doris and Eric retain a reserved life estate that permits them to continue living by the lake that they hold so dear.

Through their co-operative spirit, persistence, and love for nature, the Hopkins succeeded in achieving their goal to protect Coyote Lake and its vital buffer lands. And so, what began as a retirement place in the country, also became a priceless gift to all Albertans, and a secure home for 22 species of mammals, 266 types of plants, and 154 varieties of birds!

Common Questions

How secure is this conservation option? The new owner is responsible for ensuring that your land's natural values are protected. Accordingly, the security of donating your property to a land trust or government agency is dependent on that organization's long-term stability, resources, and commitment to conservation. It is wise to designate an alternative land trust to care for your land in the event that the original recipient organization ceases to exist. As discussed in Chapter 5, increased protection is possible by placing a conservation easement or common law covenant on title prior to donating the property.

What are the benefits? A primary benefit of donating your land to a conservation organization is the satisfaction of knowing that your land will be protected in perpetuity by experienced and dedicated individuals. Also, with most gifts of land, the donor is no longer responsible for property taxes, maintenance costs, or public liability insurance. Moreover, the donor may be able to take advantage of income tax reductions.

What are the disadvantages? Disadvantages include the loss of rights associated with land ownership, and the necessity of paying tax on capital gain (if any). However, in most cases, the income tax savings offset capital gains tax. Land transactions requiring subdivision can be a difficult and expensive process.

What are the steps in donating land? Donating land for conservation purposes involves five general steps.

<u>Step 1</u>.
Assess the natural values of your land, and determine how you want the land protected in the future. Preparing a general written stewardship plan is a useful process, for both you and the future guardian of your land.

<u>Step 2</u>.
Decide where you want to donate your property. Chapter 2 provides a useful overview of what to consider in choosing an organization. Find out whether or not the charity is setting aside endowment funds. A sound financial base is essential to meet long-term stewardship obligations and landowner liabilities. If you are interested in receiving tax benefits, be sure to select an organization that Revenue Canada considers to be a qualified recipient.

<u>Step 3</u>.
Select how you will make the donation. As noted above, there are several options available to you. It is wise to consult with your financial advisor to determine which method is most beneficial given your financial situation.

<u>Step 4</u>.
Contact the potential recipients to determine if any are willing and able to accept your gift. It is important to remember that conservation organizations, unfortunately, cannot accept all land donations. There are

costs associated with accepting a land donation (site assessment, survey, appraisal, and legal costs), and with long-term stewardship responsibilities (management plan development, property taxes, public liability insurance, signage, fencing, monitoring, enforcement, research, public education, and possibly, restoration work). Also, the organization will want to be certain that the acquisition of your land contributes to its goals. A community land trust, for instance, may accept property with locally significant values. In contrast, a larger organization may only select land that is ecologically important on an Alberta-wide, or Canada-wide scale. Yet another land trust, may only accept land that helps achieve a very specific conservation goal, such as securing elk habitat. Discuss the terms of the donation, including your wishes about future uses of the property. Also, you and the recipient will want to have your land appraised to determine its fair market value (FMV). Be sure to obtain an official income tax receipt, as you must include it with your tax return.

Step 5.

Finally, you will want to consult with your lawyer on the necessary legal procedures and to discuss a contingency plan. For example, you may want to have it stated that your property will be transferred to an alternative qualified charity, should the

original recipient fail to meet its
obligations or cease to exist.

*What are the
income tax
implications of
donating land for
conservation
purposes?*

The income tax implications of
donating land depend on the donor's
financial situation, the method of
giving, and the type of land donated.
Specific calculations are complex and
require professional advice from an
accountant or tax specialist. The
following general statements are
based on federal budget measures
announced on February 18, 1997.
Tax legislation is constantly evolving,
and consequently, each donation
must be assessed on its own merits.
To qualify for a tax receipt, the land
donation must be a voluntary transfer
for which you expect and receive
nothing of value in return.
Individuals who give a gift of land to
the Crown, a Crown Foundation,
municipality, a registered charity, or
other qualified recipient, are eligible to
claim a nonrefundable tax credit.
Corporations are eligible for a tax
deduction. The tax credit or
deduction is limited to 75% of your
net income for the year that the
donation was made. For gifts of
ecologically sensitive land, the
donation limit is 100% of your net
income for the year you transfer the
land to a qualified organization. Any
unused portions of your donation can
be carried over for up to five years. As
mentioned earlier, land (including
covenants and easements) is

considered to be capital property by Revenue Canada. When land is donated, Revenue Canada considers that the land has been disposed of, and the donor is deemed to receive the proceeds. For example, if a retired rancher donates certified ecologically significant land worth $500,000, he is deemed to have received $500,000 in proceeds. Let us say that 40 years ago it cost this landowner $100,000 to acquire the property. In this case, the donation results in a capital gain of $400,000 (fair market value minus the adjusted cost base). Seventy-five percent of the capital gain ($300,000) must be reported as income for the year of disposition. However, if we assume that the rancher's land qualifies as farm property under Revenue Canada's rules, then the available maximum accumulative capital gains deduction ($375,000) would eliminate the $300,000 taxable capital gain. In addition to qualified farm property deductions, taxable capital gain can be offset by legally devaluing the donation's value. Revenue Canada currently allows the donor to declare the deemed proceeds of disposition (the value of the gift) at any where between the gift's fair market value (FMV) and its adjusted cost base (ACB), providing the FMV is higher than the ACB. This method makes financial sense when a donor is not be able to use the full income tax receipt.

Who to Contact

For more information on taxation rules relevant to land donations, contact Revenue Canada, Charities Division.

The following organizations may accept donations of land for conservation purposes. For more information about these organizations, please see Appendix A.

- Alberta Conservation Association*
- Alberta Environmental Protection; contact your regional Natural Resources Service office
- Alberta Fish and Game Association*
- Alberta Sport, Recreation, Parks and Wildlife Foundation
- Crooked Creek Conservancy Society of Athabasca
- Ducks Unlimited Canada*
- Rocky Mountain Elk Foundation*
- Nature Conservancy of Canada*
- Southern Alberta Land Trust Society
- Trans Canada Trail Foundation*

* Denotes an organization believed to meet the criteria as a suitable recipient of ecologically sensitive lands or denotes an organization that can be helpful to contact for assistance in pursuing a donation of ecologically sensitive lands. Contact the Canadian Wildlife Service, Environment Canada for new listings.

Note: Wildlife Habitat Canada currently does not receive or manage land donations, but can facilitate such donations and provide helpful information.

Chapter 8   Generating Conservation Funds

So far we have addressed conservation options available to landowners—primarily owners of land with natural values. You need not, however, be a landowner to take direct and immediate action in saving Alberta's natural heritage. Indeed, it would be unfair to expect landowners to be the primary players in private conservancy. All Albertans must take responsibility for our common heritage and future. One important avenue open to all people is to donate cash or other assets to generate much-needed conservation funds.

With some land trusts (nonprofit conservation organizations set up to protect land for conservation purposes), your financial contribution can be directed to a specific project or specific region. Your donation can even be designated to help protect lands important to your local community. In addition, opportunities exist to have nature sanctuaries named in honour of the donor or other appropriate persons.

Through your thoughtful financial planning, you will have the satisfaction of knowing that the charity of your choice is better equipped to care for Alberta's precious natural legacy.

Conservation Funds: A Vital Component to Responsible Land Stewardship

Conservation funds enable land trusts to acquire ecologically significant lands, and to provide ongoing stewardship. Land trusts incur expenses associated with transferring title, such as legal costs, property appraisals, and land surveys. Furthermore, responsible stewardship requires ongoing financial investment. Regular site visits and monitoring, for instance, are important to ensure that conservation goals are being met. Other costly stewardship activities include conducting biological inventories, developing management plans, fencing, and sometimes, restoring disrupted ecosystems. In addition, a land trust is responsible for paying taxes on all its properties. Ideally, each nature sanctuary should have its own endowment fund.

To meet the land protection needs of each property, while keeping costs to a minimum, land trusts often work in co-operation with former landowners, local community members, volunteer naturalists, and other conservation agencies. Nonetheless, expenses usually exceed resources. Additional funding is therefore essential for long-term, responsible land stewardship.

In summary, your financial investment into a land trust is a wonderful way to make a lasting contribution to Alberta.

General Income Tax and Estate Planning Benefits

In addition to leaving a lasting natural legacy, your charitable donation can play a key role in sound financial and estate planning. With careful planning, you can optimize your gift-giving ability, minimize current income tax, and maximize the value of your estate. For example, at the time of your death, your estate must pay capital gains tax on assets that have increased in market value since you acquired them. This tax will reduce the value of your estate, leaving less money for your beneficiaries.

Through charitable giving, you can enjoy tax benefits today, and reduce, or defer, taxes on capital gains that would otherwise be payable on your death.

With a charitable donation, you can

√ obtain significant tax credits,

√ avoid needless taxation on your estate,

√ reduce or defer capital gains tax,

√ retain control of assets, and

√ enjoy a guaranteed lifetime income.

Gift Options

Revenue Canada defines a gift as a voluntary transfer of money or property for which the donor expects and receives nothing of value in return. Charitable donations may include gifts of cash, or of noncash items, such as life insurance policies, real estate, fine art, jewelry, collectibles, and other personal property.

Alberta Story

William Steel, an avid hunter and conservationist, farmed in the Eckville area for over 75 years. His concern for wildlife was shown by his retention of over 40 acres of wildlife habitat on his farm. When Mr. Steele passed away in 1995, his brother Deryl requested that all memorial contributions be made to the Buck for Wildlife Program. Through this program, the memorial funds were put to good use by supporting wildlife habitat retention and enhancement projects in Alberta.

- **Life insurance**—can be used in a variety of ways to benefit both you and the land trust of your choice. One option is to donate an existing life insurance policy that you no longer require. The tax credit will be equal to the current cash value of the insurance policy. Another way is to purchase a new policy, designate the land trust as the beneficiary, and then transfer ownership of the policy to that organization. The donor receives a tax credit for each premium paid. A third use of life insurance to generate conservation funds is by designating a land trust as beneficiary of the policy in your will. This is a very inexpensive way (via monthly or annual payments) to make a substantial future contribution. Also, if the insurance gift is separate from your estate, it is not subject to estate costs.

- **Trade lands**—are properties that lack natural values and therefore are sold by the land trust, with the donor's prior consent. The proceeds enable the land trust to purchase threatened lands of high ecological significance, or to provide ongoing care of nature sanctuaries it already owns. Residential, commercial, and developed properties can be donated as trade lands. For more de-tailed information on gifts of land, please see Chapter 7.

Ways of Giving

There are many innovative ways to make your financial contribution to a land protection fund.

How you wish to give will depend on your current and projected financial situation. You will want to consider whether you can afford to dispose of some of your assets now, or whether it is better to wait. Perhaps you want to contribute to land-saving actions, but for whatever reason are unable to do so at this time. In this case, you may want to consider having your will prepared or updated to ensure that specific assets, a portion of your estate or the residue of your estate, will be used for conservation purposes. A valid will also helps minimize complications and expenses for your estate. If you do not make a will, the government has the power to write the terms of your will for you. Consequently, an opportunity to protect Alberta's natural heritage may be lost.

If the assets you wish to donate have appreciated substantially, then you may want an option that spreads out the capital gains tax over several years. If you require additional income, you may decide to choose an option that provides a secure lifetime income.

Ways of giving include:

- **outright gifts**—a straightforward donation made during the life of the donor. This method of giving provides immediate tax advantages.

Alberta Story

Alberta ranchers Sandy and Ann Cross have given more than $10 million in land and cash to conserve wildlife habitat and to provide Albertans with conservation education opportunities. Since 1945, Dr. Sandy Cross has operated a ranch in Alberta's foothills. Once surrounded by open prairie and pockets of aspen parkland, the ranch is now within two kilometres of Calgary's city limits. The Crosses watched with concern as subdivision after subdivision carved up the foothills. This concern prompted Sandy and Ann Cross to look for a way to prevent their land from being subdivided after they no longer owned it. The solution they arrived at was to donate their land to the people of Alberta. Today, the 4,720 acre Ann and Sandy Cross Conservation Area ensures that valuable wildlife habitat is preserved in its natural state. The Area's staff and volunteers educate people about the importance of conservation.

The Sandy Cross Conservation Foundation was formed in 1996 to manage the conservation area. With the support of industry, government foundations, the Nature Conservancy of Canada, Ann and Sandy Cross, and other individuals, almost three million dollars has been raised, and an endowment fund set up to ensure ongoing care of the land. The funds have been put to good use to build a manager's residence and an education centre, to develop education programs and promotional materials, to construct and maintain 20 kilometres of hiking trails, to initiate restoration of native grasslands, and in general, to achieve long-term conservation goals. Additional funding is sought for special projects.

- **deferred gifts (bequests)**—donations given at the time of the donor's death. Charities usually prefer that you contact them before including the bequest in your will, to discuss in confidence, your donation plans. This step ensures that your wishes are clearly understood, and it verifies that the organization is willing and able to accept your gift. Bequests can generate a substantial tax credit, enabling you to give more to your beneficiaries. The tax limits for gifts made in the year of death and in the immediate taxation year is

100% of the individual's net income for those years. Any unused credit may also be carried back one year.

Two closely related ways of giving are via the charitable remainder trust and the charitable gift annuity.

- **Charitable Remainder Trust**
  With a charitable remainder trust, your donation is given to a conservation organization. The organization then transfers it to a trustee, such as a trust company. The trustee sells or manages the asset, invests the profit, and pays the annual interest to you or to a named beneficiary for a fixed period. The payments fluctuate as the trust principal grows or shrinks. At the end of the term, or on the death of the beneficiary, the remaining funds in the trust go to the named charity. As the assets in a remainder trust fall outside of the donor's estate, transfer to the charity is not delayed by the probate process, and your gift is kept private. Providing the trust is irrevocable, the donation will be eligible for a tax receipt for the gift's fair market value, less the estimated value of the payments, based on Revenue Canada actuarial tables.

- **Charitable Gift Annuity**
  A charitable gift annuity is a legally binding agreement in which a donor transfers assets to a charity, and that charity uses a portion of the donation to buy an annuity from a reputable insurance company. In the case of a land trust, the remaining funds are used by the organization to help achieve its land protection goals.
  In return for your donation, you (or your designated beneficiaries) receive regular annuity

payments for life. The payment is based on a set percentage of the donation; thus, the annuity payments remain the same, regardless of fluctuations in interest rates. A portion of your annuity income will be tax free, depending on your age at the time the annuity is purchased and the size of the annuity. You also may be eligible for an immediate, one-time tax receipt, although it will be less than if the donation were an outright gift. The reason for the reduced tax receipt is that the value of the donated property is reduced by the estimated value of the annuity payments, based on Revenue Canada actuarial tables.

Alberta Story

Joanne Hedenstrom, a former English professor, now manages a home renovation business. The majority of her renovation work occurs in rural areas where commu-

Lesley Curthoys

nity members welcome the employment opportunities, as well as the neighbourhod improvements. The renovation work not only benefits rural communities: all Albertans benefit, because business profits have enabled Joanne and her husband Don Hayden to acquired over 1200 acres of wildlife habitat. These lands will be protected in perpetuity, either by donation to conservation organizations, or by granting conservation easements. Joanne's primary interest is to conserve natural lands adjacent to national parks. These natural lands function as buffers, helping to reduce the harmful effects of toxic substances, noise, introduced species, and other disturbances that interfere with the well-being survival of our national treasures. These natural lands also function as wildlife corridors, helping wildlife to move around more safely in human-dominated landscapes. The smaller the protected area, the more vulnerable it is to outside disturbances.

Joanne has identified lands adjacent to the Waterton Lakes, Grasslands, and Point Pelee national parks, as priority areas. To ensure that her important conservation work continues, Joanne is establishing the Joanne Hedenstrom Habitat Fund. Anyone interested in contributing to this fund can contact The Calgary Foundation.

Common Questions

What are the steps involved in charitable giving?

Following the five general steps listed below may help you to maximize your charitable giving.

Step 1.
List your assets and decide if you are able to make a charitable donation.

Step 2.
Discuss your donation plans with your preferred conservation organization. Staff should be able to provide information on the best donation method to meet your personal needs, to achieve your charitable objectives, to provide more money for your beneficiaries, and to reduce your taxes. If obtaining tax benefits is important to you, be sure that the organization is a registered charity or other qualified gift recipient, as defined by Revenue Canada.

Step 3.
Consult with your legal and financial advisors.

Step 4.
Have your will professionally reviewed to incorporate your charitable giving plan. With ongoing changes in taxation legislation, it is wise to review your will on a regular basis.

Step 5.
Have a contingency plan in case arrangements made under Step 2 cease to be relevant.

What are the income tax implications of charitable giving?

Making a charitable donation may affect your tax situation. The tax implications are complex and vary depending on what you donate, the way you make the donation, and the organization to which you make the donation. Professional advice from an accountant or tax specialist is recommended. The following general statements are based on federal budget measures announced on February 18, 1997. Previously, donations to the Crown or Crown Foundations received special tax advantages. Now, with recently proposed charitable tax incentives, all gifts, with the exception of qualified ecologically sensitive land, receive equal tax treatment. If you donate capital property that has appreciated since you obtained the property, it may be subject to a tax on the capital gain. Different tax rules apply for property donated from the inventory of an artist, dealer, or collector.

Charitable Tax Incentives*

1 The general annual limit on tax credits or deductions for gifts of qualified ecologically sensitive lands is 100% of your net income for the year the land is donated or transferred to a trust. Any excess credit can be carried forward for up to five years.

2. The general annual limit on tax credits or deductions for most other types of charitable donations to qualified recipients (including the Crown and Crown Foundations) is 75% of your net income. If the value of the gift exceeds 75% of your net income in the year you donate it, you may carry the excess forward for up to five years.

3. The tax limits for gifts made in the year of death and in the immediate taxation year is 100% of the individual's net income for those years. Any unused credit may also be carried back one year.

4. To offset the capital gain from donations of highly appreciated property, the general annual limit for gifts of appreciated property has been increased by an additional 50% of the taxable capital gain.

5. With the exception of donations to private foundations, for capital gains that result from gifts of publicly traded securities to Canadian charities, the income inclusion rate has been reduced from 75% to 37.5%.

* Based on proposed amendments to the Income Tax Act

Who to Contact

For more information on planned giving, you can contact the Canadian Association of Gift Planners.

The following conservation organizations accept cash and noncash gifts for the purposes of direct land acquisitions and related stewardship projects. Additional information on each organization is provided in Appendix A.

- Alberta Conservation Association
- Alberta Fish and Game Association
- Alberta Sport, Recreation, Parks and Wildlife Foundation
- Crooked Creek Conservancy Society of Athabasca
- Ducks Unlimited Canada
- Nature Conservancy of Canada
- Rocky Mountain Elk Foundation
- Sandy Cross Conservation Foundation
- Southern Alberta Land Trust Society
- The Calgary Foundation
- Trans Canada Trail Foundation

Chapter 9   A Word about Community Land Trusts

Private conservancy is not just about protecting biological diversity. Private conservancy is also about controlling future uses of your land, safeguarding local values, and building livable communities. And who better to shape a community's future than the local people? For it is they who are sensitive to the needs of the land and the needs of their community. This is the essence of community land trusts—neighbours working together to protect land and serve their community.

Land trusts are considered the fastest growing segment of the conservation movement, with more than one new land trust forming each week in North America. As defined earlier, a land trust (or conservancy, as it is sometimes called) is a private, nonprofit organization set up to protect land. Although land trusts can operate at local, provincial, territorial, or national levels, community land trusts typically focus their efforts on protecting local natural lands and resources.

Using the conservation tools discussed in this book, these trusts help local people to protect a variety of community assets, such as ecologically sensitive lands, culturally significant areas, recreation areas, healthy watersheds, private forested lands, and agricultural lands.

Each community land trust is distinct, because it is

created by community members, and shaped by local concerns and needs. Often, community land trusts work in co-operation with local municipalities, conservation organizations, and other groups and individuals interested in protecting landscape health and community values.

Community land trusts will undoubtedly play an important role in safeguarding Alberta's healthy ecological future. It is beyond the scope of this book to address all the factors that should be considered when forming and managing a community land trust. If you are interested in forming a land trust as a positive way to shape your community's future and contribute to its well-being, you may wish to contact the groups listed at the end of this chapter. Also, *Creative Conservation: A Handbook for Ontario Land Trusts* is an excellent resource. Although the information is geared for Ontario citizens, the fundamentals can be applied to any location. Appendix B provides information on other useful land trust publications.

Alberta Story

The Crooked Creek Conservancy Society of Athabasca grew from several informal potluck supper gatherings of Crooked Creek residents who sought co-operative approaches to preserve diminishing wildlife habitat. Now, with members from a broader area, Crooked Creek Conservancy Society is bringing forward land-based conservation issues through presentations to land owners and policy makers. The Society foresees land acquisition as the next step in meeting its long-term conservation objectives.

Robert Kershaw

Alberta Story

The Southern Alberta Land Trust Society is dedicated to maintaining the ecological, agricultural, and scenic values of southern Alberta's foothill and prairie regions, such as the landscape pictured above. Its members seek to preserve the connections between people and the land which promote a sense of stewardship and underlie feelings of regional pride and cultural identity.

Who to Contact

The following organizations can provide general information on creating and managing a land trust. For more information about these organizations, please see Appendix A.

- Alberta Sport Recreation, Parks & Wildlife Foundation
- Crooked Creek Conservancy Society of Athabasca
- Land Trust Alliance
- Southern Alberta Land Trust Society
- Turtle Island Earth Stewards

Chapter 10 Making Your Vision a Reality

You may have many questions remaining as you ponder which option is best for you and your family, and for the land that you cherish. Reviewing Alberta's private conservancy options is an important first step in making your land protection goals a reality.

With information on Alberta's private conservancy options, and a clear picture of what you wish to achieve, your next step is to approach the appropriate conservation organizations. Appendix A provides contact information on all the conservation organizations mentioned in this book. These organizations are experienced in land conservation and will gladly assist you.

As is the case with most worthwhile goals, finding the right option and best partner will take time and perseverance. The important thing is to take action today, rather than jeopardizing treasured places and traditions through inaction. Don't wait till the last wetland in your area has been drained, or hope that someone else will fulfill your land protection goals.

Too often our behaviours are motivated by the myth that money, in itself, is the foundation of our well-being. Living by this myth, it is all too easy to take our natural heritage for granted, and turn a blind eye as yet another forest, wetland or prairie home is lost to "development." What we have forgotten, it seems, is that ultimately, our

well-being is derived from nature. Money, by itself, is worthless. You cannot eat it. You cannot drink it. You cannot use it to keep warm. It does not produce oxygen, purify water, or grow our food. Nor does it nourish our souls. These

gifts of life—nutrients, water, energy, air, soil, tranquillity, and companionship with our nonhuman family—are the gifts of a healthy landscape.

I have no doubt that caring for our home-place is one of the most dignified ways to make a lasting difference. Every Albertan has the power to make that difference. Whether you decide to participate in a stewardship recognition program, be party to a conservation contract, grant a conservation easement, sell land for conservation purposes, donate property to a land trust, or share your wealth to help generate conservation funds, your foresighted action to save our vanishing natural heritage will be a lasting gift to all.

Our love for life and for Alberta's natural bounty will guide us as we leave the current path of "progress at all costs" and boldly seek a more life-respecting path that safeguards our future. Best wishes in your endeavours!

Appendix A: Your Partners in Conservation

Alberta Conservation Association

4th Floor, 9920-108 Street
Mailing address
P.O. Box 40027
Baker Centre Postal Outlet
Edmonton, AB T5J 4M9
Phone: (403) 427-5192
Fax: (403) 422-6441

In 1997, the Alberta Government transferred to the Alberta Conservation Association (ACA) much of the authority and responsibility contained in the Fish and Wildlife Trust Fund Regulations, including the Wildlife Habitat Development Program (Buck for Wildlife).

Incorporated under the Alberta's Societies Act, the ACA is a separate legal entity, independent of government. The ACA is a partnership of several Alberta organizations—representing a diverse cross section of interests in conservation. These organizations include Trout Unlimited Canada, Western Walleye Council, Alberta Fish and Game Association, Professional Outfitters Association of Alberta, Alberta Trappers Association, Federation of Alberta Naturalists, and the Alberta Grand Council of Treaty 8. The ACA has been empowered under regulation to establish and collect levies on hunting and sportfishing licences, and to carry out the following functions: (1) assess, protect and enhance wildlife and fish habitats throughout the province; (2) acquire and analyse data on populations of game and nongame fish and wildlife species, including those at risk, in order to assess species and population status and to develop management strategies where necessary; and (3) carry out programs to prevent wildlife damage to agricultural crops, in some cases to compensate for livestock losses to predators, and to prevent resource violations. Partnerships, public information, and education are important elements in all three functions.

Alberta Environmental Protection

R.I.T.E. operator: 310-0000

Environmental Protection works in co-operation with provincial and local nongovernment organizations to implement private conservancy projects that meet its program priorities and objectives. Contacting your regional Natural Resources Service office is the most direct way to discuss your private conservancy goals.

Alberta Fish and Game Association

6924-104 Street
Edmonton, AB T6H 2L7
Phone: (403) 437-2342
Fax: (403) 438-6872
E-mail: office@afga.org
Web site: www.afga.org

The Alberta Fish and Game Association is a private, nonprofit organization of hunters, anglers, and outdoor enthusiasts. With local clubs in over 100 communities throughout Alberta, the Association is the province's largest conservation organization. Formed in 1909, the Association has a long history of working co-operatively with landowners, community groups, private industry, and government to ensure Alberta's fish and wildlife remain intact for future generations. Its mission is to promote, through education and programs, the conservation and utilization of fish and wildlife, and to protect and enhance the habitat they depend upon.

Alberta Sport, Recreation, Parks and Wildlife Foundation

905 Standard Life Centre
10405 Jasper Avenue
Edmonton, AB T5J 3N4
Phone: (403) 422-1097
Fax: (403) 427-5140

The Alberta Sport, Recreation, Parks and Wildlife Foundation is a crown agency. The objectives of the Foundation are (1) to develop and maintain sport programs, facilities, and services; (2) to develop and maintain recreation programs, facilities, and services; (3) to develop and maintain parks programs, facilities, and services; (4) to develop and maintain fish and wildlife programs, facilities, and services; and (5) to raise funds to be used in assisting the Foundation in carrying out its objectives. The Park and Wildlife Ventures program was established under the Foundation to acquire heritage lands and habitats by donation or purchase, and to raise funds in support of related programs and public education.

The Foundation can assist organizations in setting up land acquisition and related conservation trusts. One example of a project assisted by the Foundation is the Peaceful Valley Trust, established to fund construction of the Peaceful Valley Day Lodge and to cover long-term management and maintenance costs. Another example is This Living World Trust, established by King Motion Picture Corporation for the purpose of purchasing parcels of land to be preserved as wildlife habitat.

Sandy Cross Conservation Foundation

Ann and Sandy Cross Conservation Area
Box 20, Site 23, RR8
Calgary, AB T2J 2T9
Phone: (403) 931-3377 or 931-2042 for bookings
Fax: (403) 931-2726
E-mail: crosscons@lexicom.ab.ca
Web site: www.lexicom.ab.ca/~crosscons

The Sandy Cross Conservation Foundation was established in 1996 to manage the Ann and Sandy Cross Conservation Area. The purpose of this conservation area is to preserve wildlife habitat and to provide conservation education programs for Alberta school children and others. Funding is sought for special projects.

Canadian Association of Gift Planners

1329 Bay Street, Suite 200
Toronto, ON M5R 2C4

The purpose of the Canadian Association of Gift Planners is to support philanthropy by fostering the development and growth of gift planning. The association creates awareness, provides education, and is an advocate for charitable giving.

Crooked Creek Conservancy Society of Athabasca

P.O. Box 2072
Athabasca, AB T9S 2B6

Crooked Creek Conservancy Society of Athabasca was formed by concerned citizens in response to rapidly diminishing areas of wildlands and wildlife habitat. Members of the society are conservation-minded individuals working together to achieve long-term protection of specific areas within the Athabasca region.

The general objectives of the Society are (1) to secure,

manage, and protect land for environmental, social, or community purposes; (2) to establish community ownership and stewardship of land and its biological diversity for this and future generations; (3) to provide community awareness, education, and participation in maintaining natural habitat and wilderness areas; (4) to encourage, foster, and develop a recognition of the importance of wildlife habitat and conservation areas; (5) to express an appreciation of nature; and (6) to sell, manage, lease, mortgage, dispose of, or otherwise deal with the property of the Society.

Ducks Unlimited Canada—Alberta Office

#202, 10470-176 Street
Edmonton, AB T5S 1L3
Phone: (403) 489-2002
Fax: (403) 489-1856
E-mail: du_edmonton@ducks.ca
Web site: www.ducks.ca

Ducks Unlimited Canada (DUC) is a private, non-profit, registered charitable conservation organization with over 50 years of experience working with landowners on private conservancy projects. DUC's goal is to perpetuate and increase North American waterfowl and other wildlife species populations by enhancing and managing wetland and upland habitats, by teaching people about their value, and by supporting related scientific research. DUC promotes a multiple-use approach to conservation that benefits both the farmer and wildlife.

As part of its commitment to the North American Waterfowl Management Plan (NAWMP), Ducks Unlimited Canada operates the Alberta Prairie CARE program. Along with conserving priority wetlands and upland habitat for waterfowl and a variety of other species, the CARE program promotes agricultural techniques that improve nesting cover while protecting soil resources.

Environment Canada

Habitat Conservation Division
Canadian Wildlife Service
Environment Canada
Ottawa, ON K1A 0H3
Fax: (819) 994-4445

Edmonton Office
Phone: (403) 951-8700

Environmental Law Centre

#204, 10709 Jasper Avenue
Edmonton, AB T5J 3N3
Phone: (403) 424-5099 or
              Alberta Toll Free 1-800-661-4238
Fax: (403) 424-5133
E-mail: elc@web.net
Web site: www.web.net\~elc

The Environmental Law Centre (Alberta) Society is a nonprofit, registered Canadian charitable organization founded in 1981 in response to a need for public information and assistance on environmental law and policy. The Centre provides information for everyone, including individuals, environmental organizations, schools, universities, government, industry, and the media. The public has full access to information at the Centre library, and can attend workshops and education seminars. If needed, the lawyers at the Centre provide referrals to other lawyers and environmental specialists.

Federation of Alberta Naturalists

Box 1472
Edmonton, AB T5J 2N5
Phone: (403) 453-8629
Fax: (403) 453-8553
E-mail: fan@connect.ab.ca
Web site: www.connect.ab.ca/~fan

The Federation of Alberta Naturalists is an incorporated, nonprofit, province-wide umbrella group for natural history clubs with an elected Board of Directors. FAN's purposes are to encourage Albertans to increase their knowledge of natural history and ecological processes, to provide a unified voice for naturalists on conservation issues, to exchange data, and to promote the formation of new natural history clubs across the province.

Land Trust Alliance

1319 F Street NW
Suite 501
Washington, DC 20004-1106
Phone: (202) 638-4725
Fax: (202) 638-4730
Web site: www.lta.org

The Land Trust Alliance is a national organization of land trusts, working to ensure that land trusts have the tools and resources they need to save land through voluntary land conservation. Its expanding array of programs disseminate information, shape public policy, and make the public aware of land trusts and their role in land conservation. Books and other materials related to land conservation are available through this nonprofit organization.

Land Stewardship Centre of Canada

13 Mission Avenue
St. Albert, AB T8N 1H6
Phone: (403) 458-5700
Fax: (403) 458-0312
E-mail: lsc@compusmart.ab.ca
Web site: www.LandStewardship.org (July 1988)

The Land Stewardship Centre of Canada is an independent, nonprofit company. Its mission is to be an action-oriented centre for developing partnerships—with agriculture, industry, government, institutions, and community-based organizations—for conservation programs, projects, and exchange of knowledge that will best serve the public in achieving the vision of environmentally sustainable land management.

A major project of this organization is the Land Stewardship Resource Centre—a "one-window" electronic clearinghouse and referral service for all Albertans. The Resource Centre is a joint venture supported by major conservation agencies and more than 30 other organizations. It contains a wealth of information about land-use conservation practices, programs, agencies and the wide variety of resource materials available to the public. From farmers and ranchers, to owners of small acreages and urban yards, the Resource Centre service is designed to help landowners get the information they need for maintaining and improving the conservation of natural areas and biodiversity on their land and in their communities. The Resource Centre is scheduled to be operational in July 1998.

Nature Conservancy of Canada

National Office
Phone: 1-800-465-0029

Alberta Regional Office
Suite 3400
Petro Canada Centre
150-6th Avenue SW
Calgary, AB T2P 3Y7
Phone: (403) 294-7064
Fax: (403) 265-8263
E-mail: nature@natureconservancy.ca

The Nature Conservancy of Canada (NCC), founded in 1963, is a nonadvocacy, nonpolitical conservation group dedicated to purchasing natural areas of ecological significance, outstanding beauty, and educational interest. The NCC works co-operatively with individuals, communities, businesses, schools, and governments. Specifically, the mission for the NCC's Alberta regional office is to work in co-operation with the people of Alberta to conserve privately owned natural landscapes, principally ranchlands, east of the Rockies.

Red Deer River Naturalists

Box 785
Red Deer, AB T4N 5H2
Phone: (403) 347-8200 (answering machine)

The Red Deer River Naturalists Society (RDRN) was established in 1906. The RDRN society is a registered nonprofit society and is a member of the Federation of Alberta Naturalists. The society's purposes are to foster knowledge and appreciation of natural history; to support conservation measures dealing with our environment, wildlife, and natural resources; to cooperate with other clubs and organizations having similar views and objectives; and to support the Federation of Alberta Naturalists.

In addition to operating the Habitat Steward program and NatureScape Alberta, RDRN offers public programs, helps co-ordinate the Christmas and spring species counts, sponsors volunteer awards, provides public information about environmental issues, and produces a membership newsletter ten times a year.

Revenue Canada

Charities Division
400 Cumberland Street
Ottawa, ON K1A 0L5
Phone: 1-800-267-2384

Rocky Mountain Elk Foundation

P.O. Box 940
Rocky Mountain House, AB T0M 1T0
Phone: (403) 845-6492 or 1-800-563-7633
Fax: (403) 845-2410
E-mail: rmefc@telusplanet.net
Web Site: http://www.rmef.org

The Rocky Mountain Elk Foundation (RMEF) is an international, nonprofit wildlife conservation organization. The foundation's mission is to ensure the future of elk, other wildlife and their habitat. RMEF's conservation programs include habitat conservation, wildlife management, research, and conservation education. These programs are funded through the North American Habitat Fund.

To achieve its mission, the RMEF purchases wildlife habitat, receives land donations, and holds conservation easements on private lands. In most cases, the RMEF does not retain ownership of acquired lands. Instead, it may donate, resell or lease acquired habitat to the provincial government or a private conservation partner, who is then responsible for managing the land.

Southern Alberta Land Trust Society

P.O. 327
Pincher Creek, AB T0K 1W0
Phone/Fax: (403) 627-4230
E-mail: salts@canuck.com

The Southern Alberta Land Trust Society (SALTS) is a grassroots, nonprofit organization composed of ranchers and professional natural resource managers dedicated to maintaining the ecological, agricultural, and scenic values of southern Alberta's foothill and prairie regions.

SALTS promotes a landscape approach to conservation by coordinating the protection of agricultural lands and natural areas. Its conservation efforts reflect the diverse environmental, economic, cultural, and aesthetic values present in ranchlands and open spaces. SALTS strives to maintain the integrity and productivity of the land base through the continuation of compatible land uses. Its goals include preserving the connections between people and the land which promote a sense of stewardship and underlie feelings of regional pride and cultural identity. SALTS is locally based, allowing the organization to be effective in the development of conservation projects on farms and ranches through our understanding of the needs and concerns of individual property owners and the community. To accomplish its goals, SALTS functions both independently and in collaboration with like-minded groups.

The Calgary Foundation

Suite 1920 Aquitaine Tower
540-5th Avenue SW
Calgary, AB T2P 0M2
Phone: (403) 264-1662
Fax: (403) 265-0152
E-mail: calfound@cadvision.com

The Calgary Foundation is a public charity that was formed in 1955 by a group of community-minded citizens to meet various social, cultural, educational, health care, and development priorities in Calgary, and the surrounding area. A primary focus of the foundation is to build endowment funds, established by donors to support the long-term growth and well-being of the Calgary community. The Calgary Foundation exists to encourage the increased flow of resources to build the Calgary community, to create and manage permanent endowment funds that stabilize and strengthen the city of Calgary for the long term, and to respond creatively to pressing and yet changing issues by using currently available discretionary dollars.

Contributions to the Joanne Hedenstrom Habitat Fund (discussed in Chapter 8) can be made through this Foundation.

Trans Canada Trail Foundation

1-800-465-3636
Alberta contact: Alberta TrailNet
11759 Groat Road
Edmonton AB T5M 3K6
Phone: (403) 287-0795
Fax: (403) 243-0530
Web Site: www.tctrail.ca

The Trans Canada Trail Foundation is an independent, registered charity organization with its own Corporate Charter, operating by-laws, and Board of Directors. The mission of the Foundation is to promote and co-ordinate the planning, design, and building of a continuous, shared-use recreation trail that winds its way through every province and territory.

Alberta TrailNet is developing associations with local communities, government organizations, and interested groups and individuals throughout Alberta to help plan and construct the Trans Canada Trail.

Turtle Island Earth Stewards

Box 3308
Salmon Arm, BC V1E 4S1
Phone: (250) 832-3993
Fax: (250) 832-9942
E-mail: ties@jetstream.net
Web Site: http://www.landtrust.org/turtleisland

Turtle Island Earth Stewards (TIES) is a grassroots, nonprofit, charitable conservation organization. Since 1975, it has been involved in community service and has helped to place lands and forests in trust. TIES encourages the private stewardship of all types of land, including agricultural land, managed forests, and natural areas. If you own land and want to leave a living legacy for future generations, TIES can help you place your land in trust.

The Turtle Island Group, the consulting arm of the Turtle Island Earth Stewards, has extensive experience in establishing community land trusts and other land stewardship approaches valuable to community development in urban and rural settings. An information package on the group's consulting services is available on request.

Wildlife Habitat Canada

Suite 200
7 Hinton Avenue North
Ottawa, ON K1Y 4P1
Phone: (613) 722-2090
Fax: (613) 722-3318
E-mail: jladd.whc.org

Founded in 1984, Wildlife Habitat Canada (WHC) is a prominent national leadership resource for Canadian wildlife habitat conservation. A nonprofit foundation, WHC builds cooperative partnerships with governments, nongovernment organizations, industries, corporations, and private citizens to protect, enhance, and restore wildlife habitat throughout Canada

WHC has a granting program which supports habitat conservation activities at local, provincial, and national levels. Since 1985, WHC has raised and awarded over $25 million to habitat conservation projects. WHC is particularly interested in developing programs which encourage voluntary conservation or stewardship of natural resources. In addition to its granting program, WHC also provides perspectives and advice to governments on policy and legislation. Information on WHC and its programs is available by contacting the foundation.

Appendix B Useful Resources

Community Land Trusts

Aberley, Doug (ed.). 1993. *Boundaries of Home: Mapping for Local Empowerment.* New Society Publishers. Gabriola Island, British Columbia.

Hilts, S and R. Reid. 1993. *Creative Conservation: A Handbook for Ontario Land Trust.* Federation of Ontario Naturalists. Don Mills, Ontario.

Hough, Michael. 1990. *Out of Place: Restoring Identity to the Regional Landscape.* Yale University Press. New Haven.

Turtle Island Earth Stewards 1996. *Guide to Forming Community Land Trusts.* Turtle Island Earth Stewards. Salmon Arm, British Columbia.

The Land Trust Alliance. 1990. *Starting a Land Trust: A Guide to Forming a Land Conservation Organization.* The Land Trust Alliance. Washington, D.C.

Conservation Easements and Other Legal Tools

Attridge, I. 1996. *Conservation Easement Valuation and Taxation in Canada.* North American Wetlands Conservation Council (Canada). Toronto, Ontario.

Findlay, B. and A. Hillyer. 1994. *Here Today, Here Tomorrow: Legal Tools for the Voluntary Protection of Private Land in British Columbia.* West Coast Environmental Law Research Foundation. Vancouver, British Columbia.

Kwasniak, A. 1996. *Conservation Easement Guide for Alberta.* Environmental Law Centre. Edmonton, Alberta.

Lind, B. 1991. *The Conservation Easement Stewardship Guide: Designing, Monitoring, and Enforcing Easements.* Land Trust Alliance. Washington, D.C.

Tingley, D., F.P. Kirby, and R.D. Hupfer. 1986. *Conservation Kit: A Legal Guide to Private Conservancy.* Environmental Law Centre. Edmonton, Alberta.

Current State of Our Natural Heritage

Hummel, M. (ed.). 1995. *Protecting Canada's Endangered Spaces: An Owner's Manual.* Key Porter Books Ltd. Toronto, Ontario.

Stewardship Guides

Adams, B. and L. Fitch. 1995. *Caring for the Green Zone: Riparian Areas and Grazing Management.* Published by and available from the "Cows and Fish Partners" (Alberta Riparian Habitat Management Project): Alberta Cattle Commission; Trout Unlimited Canada; Canadian Cattleman's Association; Alberta Environmental Protection; Alberta Agricultural, Food and Rural Development; and Department of Fisheries and Oceans.

Trottier, G.C. 1992. *A Landowner's Guide: Conservation of Canadian Prairie Grasslands.* Minister of Supplies and Services Canada. Environment Canada. Western and Northern Region.

Prairie Conservation Forum. 1997. *Alberta Prairie Conservation Action Plan.* Prairie Conservation Forum. Lethbridge, Alberta.

Bradley, C. and C. Wallis. 1996. *Prairie Ecosystem Management: An Alberta Perspective.* Prairie Conservation Forum. Occasional Paper Number 2.

Glossary

actuarial table—a table that presents statistically based life expectancy information

adjusted cost base (ACB)—a property's value when inherited, or a property's value when purchased, plus acquisition costs and certain capital expenditures

biodiversity or **biological diversity**—the variety of life, and the ecological processes and cycles that link the well-being and survival of all life forms, including humans

boreal—the natural region covering most of northern Alberta and characterized by spruce, poplar, and pine tree stands, interspersed with wetlands

buffer lands—natural landscapes that filter out or reduce the harmful influences of toxic substances, noise, introduced species, and other disturbances

capital property—defined by Revenue Canada as "any property of value that you buy for investment purposes or to earn income. Some common examples of capital property include your home, your cottage, securities such as stocks and bonds, and land, buildings, and equipment that you use in a business or rental operation."

conservation easement—a voluntary legal agreement between a landowner and a qualified organization whereby any registered landowner is able to retain ownership of the land while transferring specific rights to its uses to an easement-holding organization, for the purpose of protecting the land's natural values on a long-term or permanent basis

ecologically significant land (also called an **ecological gift**)—land certified by the Minister of the Environment as important to preserving Canada's environmental heritage

ecosystem—an interconnected system of living and non-living forms, and the ecological processes that link them

endowment—a permanent fund established to provide financial support for a specific project or purpose

gift—defined by Revenue Canada as a "voluntary transfer of property for which the donor expects and receives nothing of value in return"

grantee—the recipient of a conservation easement; also called the holder of the easement

grantor—the person who grants a conservation easement

grassland—the natural region of Alberta characterized by unbroken native prairie

in perpetuity—forever

land trust—in the context of this book, a land trust is a nonprofit organization established to acquire and protect land or interests in land (such as conservation easements) for conservation purposes

monitoring—recording landscape changes and overall landscape health, as indicated by such things as water quality and quantity, biodiversity, soil productivity, and lack of pollutants

Natural Area—in Alberta, a Crown land that falls in the middle range of conservation lands between fairly strict protected lands (such as ecological reserves), and intensively developed lands (such as provincial recreation areas)

natural wildlife corridor—areas that facilitate natural wildlife movement, dispersal, and genetic interchange

occupiers' liability—the Alberta *Occupiers' Liability Act* imposes a duty of care on private landowners or others with an interest in land (such as a tenant or holder of a conservation easement) to take reasonable care to ensure that visitors to the property will be safe in using premises under that person's control

parkland—the natural region of Alberta occurring between the open grasslands in southern Alberta and the boreal forests in northern Alberta. Parkland is characterized by a mosaic of wetlands, fescue grasslands, and aspen groves on a gently rolling landscape

private conservancy—the voluntary involvement of citizens, nongovernment organizations, and corporations in natural heritage protection

riparian areas—places where land and water meet, such as along streams, lakes, and rivers and their floodplains

watershed—the flow and collection of water from the highest to the lowest points of land, influencing all aspects of natural systems from soil productivity, nutrient cycling, vegetation types, and wildlife inhabitants, to the location and potential of human communities

Bibliography

Adams, B. and L. Fitch. 1995. *Caring for the Green Zone: Riparian Areas and Grazing Management*. Published by Alberta Cattle Commission; Trout Unlimited Canada; Canadian Cattleman's Association; Alberta Environmental Protection; Alberta Agricultural, Food and Rural Development; and Department of Fisheries and Oceans.

Alberta Environmental Protection. 1996. Spring/Summer. *Buck for Wildlife Newsletter*. Alberta Environmental Protection, Natural Resources Service. Alberta.

Alberta Environmental Protection 1996. Fall/Winter. *Buck for Wildlife Newsletter*. Alberta Environmental Protection, Natural Resources Service. Alberta.

Alberta Environmental Protection and Alberta Conservation Association. 1997. Spring/Summer. *Buck for Wildlife Newsletter*. Alberta Conservation Association and Alberta Environmental Protection, Natural Resources Service. Alberta.

Alberta Recreation, Parks and Wildlife Foundation. (no date) *Our Legacy*. Volume XIII, Issue I.

Brenneman, R. and S. Bates (eds.). 1984. *Land Saving Action*. Island Press. Covelo, California.

Canadian Association of Gift Planners. *Planned Giving: Your Lasting Gift*. Magazine published by the Canadian Association of Gift Planners. Toronto, Ontario.

Catterton, J. L. 1990. Appraising Conservation Easement Gifts: A Primer for Landowners. *Exchange* 4. (Land Trust Alliance). Summer 1990.

Coaldale Ecology Club, Lethbridge Naturalist Society, South Country Community Association, and the Southern Alberta Environmental Group. 1993. *South Country Protected Areas Project: Phase One Summary Report.* Environmental Resource Centre. Lethbridge, Alberta.

Coaldale Ecology Club, Lethbridge Naturalist Society, South Country Community Association, and the Southern Alberta Environmental Group. 1995. *South Country Protected Areas Project: Phase Two Stakeholder Contacts Process Report.* Environmental Resource Centre. Lethbridge, Alberta.

Deans, K. (ed.). 1993. *Conservation Options: A Landowner's Guide.* Land Trust Alliance. Washington, D.C.

Denhez, Marc. 1992. *You Can't Give It Away: Tax Aspects of Ecologically Sensitive Lands.* Issue Paper No. 1992-4. North American Wetlands Conservation Council (Canada). Ottawa, Ontario.

Environment Canada. 1997. *Donation of Ecologically Sensitive Land in Canada: Implementing New Provisions of the Income Tax Act of Canada.* Revised Information Circular No. 2. Canadian Wildlife Service. Ottawa, Ontario. Revised January 3, 1997.

Environment Canada. 1997. (compiled by C. Rubec) Ecological Gifts: Implementing Provisions of the Income Tax Act of Canada. Canadian Wildlife Service, Environment Canada. Ottawa, Ontario. Revised September 3, 1997

Environment Canada. 1997. *List of Certification Authorities and Qualified Recipient Charities and Municipalities for Donation of Ecologically Sensitive Lands.* Revised Information Circular No. 3. Canadian Wildlife Service. Ottawa, Ontario.

Fenton, J. and J. Lilley. 1996. *Annotated Guide to Alberta's Legislation, Policies and Programs Affecting Wildlife Habitat.* Alberta NAWMP Centre. North American Wildlife Management Plan. Edmonton, Alberta.

Findlay, B. and A. Hillyer. 1994. *Here Today, Here Tomorrow: Legal Tools for the Voluntary Protection of Private Land in British Columbia.* West Coast Environmental Law Research Foundation. Vancouver, British Columbia.

Flemming, L. 1995. Coyote Lake a Haven for Life. *This Week.* Friday, March 24:15.

Katakis, M. 1993. *Sacred Trusts: Essays on Stewardship and Responsibility.* Mercury House. San Francisco, California.

Hilts, S., M. Kirk, R. Reid and contributors. 1986. *Islands of Green: Natural Heritage Protection in Ontario.* Ontario Heritage Foundation. Toronto, Ontario.

Hilts, S. and T. Moull. 1988. *Protecting Ontario's Natural Heritage Through Private Stewardship.* Department of Land Resource Science, University of Guelph. Guelph, Ontario.

Hilts, S. 1990. Private Stewardship: Its Beginnings and Use Across Canada. In Nelson, J.G. and S. Woodley (eds.). *Heritage Conservation and Sustainable Development.* University of Waterloo. Waterloo, Ontario.

Hilts, S. and R. Reid. 1993 *Creative Conservation: A Handbook for Ontario Land Trust.* Federation of Ontario Naturalists. Don Mills, Ontario.

Hoose, P. M. 1981. *Building an Ark: Tools for the Preservation of Natural Diversity Through Land Protection.* Island Press. Covelo, California.

Hough, M. 1990. *Out of Place: Restoring Identity to the Regional Landscape.* Yale University Press. New Haven.

Hummel, Monte (ed.). 1989. *Endangered Spaces: The Future for Canada's Wilderness.* Key Porter Books Ltd. Toronto, Ontario.

Hummel, M. (ed.). 1995. *Protecting Canada's Endangered Spaces: An Owner's Manual.* Key Porter Books Ltd. Toronto, Ontario.

Hunt, C. *Partners in Land Acquisition.* (no date) Hunt Consulting. Copies available from the Alberta Fish and Game Association, Edmonton, Alberta.

Island Nature Trust. 1989. *Private Stewardship: The Landowner's Options.* Island Nature Trust. Charlottetown, Prince Edward Island.

Kwasniak, A. (ed.). 1994. *Private Conservancy: The Path to Law Reform.* Environmental Law Centre. Edmonton, Alberta.

Kwasniak, A. 1997. *Conservation Easement Guide for Alberta.* Environmental Law Centre. Edmonton, Alberta.

Land Trust Alliance. 1994. *Economic Benefits of Land Protection.* Washington, D.C.

Layard, N. and E. Neely (eds.). 1992. *Land for Nature Forum: Tools and Mechanisms.* Federation of British Columbia Naturalists. Vancouver, British Columbia.

Milne, J. E. 1984. The Landowner's Options. In Brenneman, R. and S. Bates (eds.), *Land Saving Action.* Island Press. Covelo, California.

Milne, J. E. 1985. *The Landowner's Options: A Guide to the Voluntary Protection of Land in Maine.* Maine State Planning Office. Maine.

Montana Land Reliance and Land Trust Exchange. 1982. *Private Options: Tools and Concepts for Land Conservation.* Island Press. Covelo, California.

Mitchell, G. 1996. *The Alberta Environmental Directory: An Annotated Guide to Alberta's Environmental Organizations and Agencies.* 8th ed. The Pembina Institute for Appropriate Development. Drayton Valley, Alberta.

Nature Conservancy of Canada. 1997. *The Habitat Guardian: A Financial Planning Newsletter for Friends of the Nature Conservancy of Canada.* Spring 1997. Nature Conservancy of Canada. Toronto, Ontario.

Nature Conservancy of Canada. 1997. *The Nature Legacy Program.* Nature Conservancy of Canada. Toronto, Ontario.

Palmer, C. and D. Hjertaas. 1989. Operation Burrowing Owl. Pp. 236-237 In Holroyd, G.L., G. Burns, H.C. Smith. (eds.). Natural History Occasional Paper No. 15 *Proceedings for the Second Endangered Species and Prairie Conservation Workshop.* Alberta Provincial Museum. Edmonton, Alberta.

Pauley, G. 1996. *Landowners' Attitudes Toward the Use of Conservation Easements to Preserve Wildlife Habitat and Agricultural Land.* Faculty of Environmental Design, University of Calgary. Calgary, Alberta.

Pearman, M. 1989. Balanced Land Use on Private Lands. In Holroyd, G.L., G. Burns, H.C. Smith. (eds.). Natural History Occasional Paper No. 15 *Proceedings for the Second Endangered Species and Prairie Conservation Workshop.* Alberta Provincial Museum. Edmonton, Alberta.

Revenue Canada. 1996. *Gifts and Income Tax.* P113(E) Rev. 96 Charities Division, Revenue Canada, Ottawa, Ontario.

Revenue Canada. 1996. *Supporting Canada's Charities.* 96-244. Charities Division, Revenue Canada, Ottawa, Ontario.

Ruiter Valley Land Trust. 1992. *Report on the First Interprovincial Conference on Land Trusts.* Ruiter Valley Land Trust. Dunkin, Quebec.

Russell, J.S. 1995. Land Trusts and Community Planning: Reaåching a Broader Constituency. 4(6) *Exchange.* (Land Trust Alliance). Winter 1995.

Schauffler, F. M. 1994. *Conservation Options: A Guide for Maine Landowners.* Maine Coast Heritage Trust. Brunswick, Maine.

Small, S. J. 1992. *Preserving Family Lands: Essential Tax Strategies for the Landowner.* Landowner Planning Center. Boston, Massachusetts.

Smith, C. 1997. Private Conservancy: A Personal Experience. 1(2) *Encompass* 18.

Thomas, R. G. 1997. Fragile Future: Can Alberta's Forest Birds Survive in a Fragmented World? 1(2) *Encompass* 6.

Tingley, D. F., P. Kirby, and R. D. Hupfer. 1986. *Conservation Kit: A Legal Guide to Private Conservancy.* Environmental Law Centre. Edmonton, Alberta.

Trottier, G., C. 1992. *A Landowner's Guide Conservation of Canadian Prairie Grasslands.* Minister of Supply and Services Canada, Environment Canada. Western and Northern Region.

The Trust for Public Land. 1995. *Doing Deals: A Guide to Buying Land for Conservation.* Land Trust Alliance and The Trust for Public Land, Washington, D.C.

Turtle Island Earth Stewards. 1996. *Guide to Forming Community Land Trusts.* Turtle Island Earth Stewards. Salmon Arm, British Columbia.

Van Patter, M. and S. Hilts. 1990. Natural Heritage Protection: Voluntary Stewardship or Planning Control? 30(5) *Plan Canada* 20.

Van Patter, M., H. Geerts, and S. Hilts. 1990. Enhancing private stewardship. 10(3) *Natural Areas Journal* 121.

von Hauff, Donna (ed.). 1992. *Alberta's Parks: Our Legacy.* Alberta Recreation, Parks and Wildlife Foundation. Edmonton, Alberta.

Wark, R. R., and K. S. Wark. 1996. *The Story of the Peaceful Valley Project.* Alberta Sport, Recreation, Parks and Wildlife Foundation. Edmonton, Alberta.

Wildlife Habitat Canada. 1987. *Wildlife Conservation on Private Lands.* Proceedings of the Private Stewardship/Landowner Contact Workshop. Reference Paper No. 1. Wildlife Habitat Canada. Ottawa, Ontario.

Wright, J. B. and S. G. Hilts. 1993. An Overview of Voluntary Approaches to Landscape Conservation in the United States and Canada. 11(3) *The Operational Geographer* 10.

World Wildlife Fund Canada and Forestry, Lands and Wildlife, Fish and Wildlife Division. 1992. *Conservation and Management Strategy for Riparian Forests in Southern Alberta.* Alberta Energy/Forestry, Lands and Wildlife. Calgary, Alberta.

Yogis, J. A. 1990. *Canadian Law Dictionary.* Barron's Educational Series Inc. Toronto, Ontario.

Provincial Statutes

Environmental Protection and Enhancement Act, S.A. 1992, c. E-13

Land Titles Act, R.S.A. 1980, c.L-5

Municipal Government Act, S.A. 1994, c.M-26.1

Occupiers' Liability Act, R.S.A. 1980, c.o-3

Societies Act, R.S.A. 1980, c.S-18